ENGLISH ENAMEL BOXES

ENGLISH ENAMEL BOXES

From the Eighteenth to the Twentieth Centuries

Susan Benjamin

LITTLE, BROWN

For Bill

End papers: From *The Ladies Amusement* or *Whole Art of Japanning Made Easy* issued around 1758-62 by Robert Sayer of Fleet Street, London

Title page: Four boxes made in the Midlands around 1770. They illustrate the manner in which the English eighteenth-century invention of transfer-printing enabled designs on enamels to be duplicated. The two engravings which decorate these boxes are *A Gallant offering a rose* by an unknown artist and *The Haymakers* by Robert Hancock (c. 1731-1817). The smallest box is 5.8 cm (2¼ ins) across. (Halcyon Days)

A Little Brown Book

© 1978 Susan Benjamin

First published in Great Britain in 1978
by Orbis Publishing Limited, London

Reprinted 1980, 1981, 1983, 1984

Published in 1987
by Macdonald & Co (Publishers) Ltd

This edition published in 1993
by Little Brown and Company (UK)

Printed in China

ISBN 0 316 90939 4

Little Brown and Company (UK)
Brettenham House
Lancaster Place
London
WC2E 7EN

Contents

La Prise de Tabac by John James Chalon (1778–1854). (Mansell Collection)

Foreword

What follows is a work which springs from the author's deep affection for her subject—it is quite innocent of the tell-tale marks of the professional researcher who has simply carried out a commission. It was, I think, a driving curiosity, amounting almost to an obsession which has enabled her to explain so clearly and so readably the complicated techniques involved in the making of the engaging enamelled objects which form the theme of this book.

The history and social significance of the small decorative enamelled English box in particular, is discussed with perception and scholarship. In explaining how Battersea was not after all the source of all English painted and transfer-printed enamels—a misconception widely held until the publication of Bernard Rackham's Schreiber Catalogue of 1924—we are told of the various manufactories functioning all over the country, and in attributing the origins of particular examples the author displays a modesty only to be found in one who is sure of her ground—she writes: 'a conclusion reached today may be amended in the light of new evidence.' Most readers in spite of this disclaimer, will feel entirely comfortable and safe in Susan Benjamin's hands.

Although the subject of the book is by no means confined to English boxes, but encompasses a far wider range to include countless personal accoutrements and decorative items appropriate to the enameller's craft all over Europe, boxes do provide the most important single theme. They have, from the earliest times, exerted an almost hypnotic fascination upon our imagination; the invention of the box itself springs from an instinct to hide things away, representing a sublimation of a secret desire to return to our pre-natal warmth and security. If this is indeed so, the charming little motto box—so many of which were made in the South Staffordshire centres of Bilston and Wednesbury from about 1770, successfully answered this psychological need.

Proudly flaunting their topographical, sentimental or bawdy tags across gently *bombé* lids reading for example: 'A trifle from Bognor Regis', 'When this you see pray think on me, Th'o many miles we distant be' or perhaps 'In love at night is my delight', they still play a special private ambassadorial role today. This is a coherent and thoughtful book full of an enthusiasm which has been transmitted with style.

A. KENNETH SNOWMAN, LONDON, 1978

In 1759 John Taylor, a Birmingham manufacturer of enamels, observed that some 40 Frenchmen were constantly employed drawing and designing in Birmingham. The work of a number of these artists no doubt contributed considerably towards the French influence in the design and decoration of English eighteenth-century enamels made in the Midlands.
Top: Groups of figures from two famous paintings by Jean

Antoine Watteau (1684–1721) were used to decorate this magnificent enamel casket. The design on the lid is transfer-printed in red and overpainted. The two swans in the foreground typify 'The Swan Group' which is referred to on page 69. Inside the lid there is a small painting in red monochrome after François Boucher's (1703–1770) *Pensent-ils au Raisin* which depicts a youth and a shepherdess.
The chased gilt metal mounts

are very fine. The casket was probably made in Birmingham in the mid 1750s. Length 18.8 cm (7½ ins) (Victoria & Albert Museum)
Details taken from prints of the two Watteau paintings are shown below the casket.
Above left: *Amusements Champêtres*, engraved by Benoit Audran.
Above right: *La Cascade*, engraved by Gerard Jean-Baptiste Scotin. (British Museum)

Introduction

Chelsea porcelain *bonbonnières* and scent bottles,
Continental painted snuff-boxes and works by
famous French artists were among the principal
influences on the design and decoration of
eighteenth-century English enamels.

THE SMALL enamel box is one of the most appealing of all
the delicate products of Georgian craftsmanship. Intended primarily to contain snuff or patches (beauty spots),
it became almost a necessity to the sophisticates of the
eighteenth century for whom snuff-taking and the applying
of patches, to complete the perfect toilette, were everyday
rituals. The exquisite gold and enamel boxes being made at
that time by Parisian and London jewellers and goldsmiths
were, however, beyond the reach of the majority of the merchants and shopkeepers who constituted a rapidly prospering
bourgeoisie in England. These were the people who were
quick to appreciate the novelty and charm of the little enamel
box with its decoration inspired by (and frequently copied
from) the works of famous French artists such as Watteau,
Lancret, Boucher and Claude Lorraine.

Various methods of enamelling have been employed in the
decorative arts throughout the ages but a technique dating
from the late fifteenth century—that of painting with enamels
—led to greater artistic freedom than had previously been
possible. During the first half of the eighteenth century the
production of painted enamel on copper snuff-boxes flourished
on the Continent. The important development which formed
the basis for the era of English enamels from *circa* 1750 to *circa*
1840 was the advent of transfer-printing, although finely
painted enamels were also widely produced in England during
that period. Transfer-printed enamels were regarded as
a novelty by fashionable Georgian society. In September
1755, Horace Walpole wrote to a friend: 'I shall send you a
trifling snuff-box, only for a sample of the new manufacture
at Battersea, which is done with copper plates.'[1]

The fame of the Battersea enterprise was such that for
almost two centuries it was credited with having made most
English enamels. In recent years, however, it has become
clear that Battersea produced only a small, select minority;
elsewhere in London, in Birmingham, Bilston and other South
Staffordshire areas, copper enamelling was being carried out

from the 1740s; it was from these places that the majority of painted and transfer-printed enamels emanated.

The taste for charming and delicately decorated useful objects dated from around the early Georgian period when those of highest privilege and wealth throughout Europe patronized the top French jewellers and enamellers. Exquisite enamel paintings on gold watch cases, boxes, scent bottles, *carnets de bal*, and on many other objects, which featured Boucher nymphs, floral sprays, birds, cupids, fruit and animals, with possibly also a personalized inscription, such as '*Souvenir de l'amitié*' were exchanged as tokens of esteem by the aristocracy.

Later as the craft spread to England, although precious gold enamelled *bibelots* continued to be made, increasingly in the case of a wide range of articles the base was no longer of thin gold but of copper. As the eighteenth century progressed these *objets de vitrine* enamelled on copper were highly esteemed as suitable and desirable alternatives to the more formal, more costly products of the goldsmith's workshop. In addition to snuff-boxes and patch-boxes, *bonbonnières* (to hold sweetmeats or cachous to sweeten the breath), scent bottles, bodkin cases, *étuis* (containing such things as scissors, tweezers, a tiny spoon, a pencil, an ivory memorandum slip) and other trifles known as 'toys' were made to please the Georgian élite. The word toy was not used to describe a plaything but referred to an adult trinket of a frivolous nature. According to Eric Benton, who has researched English enamels for many years, 'toy' or 'toie' was first used in the early days of the Midland metal trade as a variant of 'tie' or 'tye' meaning a small metal box or casket. More useful objects such as inkstands, salt cellars and tea caddies were also made in enamel.

The period of English copper enamels covers almost a hundred years (from the late 1740s), and even though a wonderful variety of magnificent articles was produced during those years, to the entirely uninitiated observer neither the larger, more spectacular articles, such as candlesticks and caskets, nor the majority of intricate smaller pieces declare themselves at first glance to be enamels. They look almost like porcelain from such places as Mennecy, Sèvres, Meissen or Chelsea. But if there is one small item which is instantly recognizable by all as an English enamel it is the unassuming, very small box bearing an inscription.

The little motto box, measuring less than five centimetres (two inches) across, was unique inasmuch as its like had not previously existed. It was incomparable in the very simplicity of its style, which was perhaps the reason for its immense popularity. Early examples, dating from about 1770, were beautifully executed with elegant calligraphy and painted scenes or finely drawn transfer-printed motifs and borders. Their sentimental, romantic or philosophical messages, such as 'If you love me Don't deceive me', 'Love and be Happy', and 'Live and Let Live', added to the intimacy of presents given to friends and lovers. Later when the spa and resort trade was being catered for, it was the fashion to bring home a souvenir inscribed, for example, 'A trifle from Tunbridge Wells'. From 1790 onwards the quality of enamels deteriorated rapidly as manufacturers rushed to capitalize on the ever-increasing demand for inexpensive trifles which could be exchanged as keepsakes. By the early 1800s the little boxes with messages had become quickly-made, shoddy objects with scant artistic merit. But the years have endowed even these with a naive charm and today they are almost as eagerly sought by collectors as the most perfect example of a Battersea transfer-print by Ravenet, or a sumptuous casket made when the craft in Staffordshire was at its apogee in the 1770s.

By the 1830s, the English enamelling industry had all but ceased. Small manufacturing units in England were finding it difficult to survive in the face of the Industrial Revolution which created the dominant force of heavy industry. Bankruptcy notices of sales of stocks abounded in the press. The slump, for small businesses, was brought about as a direct result of the Napoleonic Wars, which had closed the door on English exports to the Continent. Also, as artistic standards deteriorated enamels had ceased to be fashionable and the enamellers could not compete with the profusion of ceramics, glass and all types of metal goods which were flooding the market. The last recorded nineteenth-century enameller stopped trading in 1840.

English enamels do not bear the maker's marks and on only a few can an artist's signature be found. One must therefore learn to distinguish them from Continental examples of a similar style and period, and to spot late nineteenth- and twentieth-century copies.

To be able to isolate one category of enamels from another demands considerable study of museum and private collections and, ideally, guidance from an expert—although it cannot be stressed too strongly that experts differ in their views on sources of manufacture. Little written information on the subject has come to light and enamels so rarely bear any indication of origin that a conclusion reached today may be amended in the light of new evidence. The illustrations which follow will assist collectors in their endeavours.

fig . 1 .

fig . 2 .

fig . 1 .

fig . 2 . fig . 3 . fig . 4 .

fig . 5 .

fig . 6 .

fig . 7 .

fig . 8 .

fig . 9 .

fig . 10 .

1   2   3   4 Pieds .

History and Techniques of Enamelling

Throughout the ages enamel has been prized by decorators of *objets d'art*.

Left: Diderot's *Encyclopédie des sciences, des arts et des métiers* was published in Paris during the 14 years from 1751. The encyclopedia includes a 12-page entry on *Émail, branche de la Verrerie* which gives a comprehensive description of enamelling techniques and formulae. In 1765, Diderot also published volume IV of the *Recueil des planches sur les Arts Libéraux et les Arts Méchaniques avec leur explication* from which the engraving on the facing page is taken. This illustrates how a painter of enamels can work in a tranquil atmosphere away from the hurly-burly of the factory. The artist seen here in his elegant studio has the two basic requirements: a good light and a fireplace in which to stand a small kiln for firing the decorated enamels. Beneath the picture of the studio are section drawings of the type of coal-burning muffle-kiln used in the eighteenth century. Diderot's illustrations convey the immense charm of the period without in any way detracting from the precise technical information for which his work is famous. (Victoria & Albert Museum)

Above: A Chinese *cloisonné* bowl, decorated on the outside with Buddhist lions chasing ribboned brocade balls among Taoist auspicious symbols, in coloured enamels on a blue ground. Around the foot there is a border of lappets in white and red; the domed base has a large red peony and foliage and the inside of the bowl is decorated with dappled horses running across waves with clouds swirling above their heads. The lip has a band of flowers on a white ground. Sixteenth century. Diameter 20 cm (8 ins) (Bluett & Sons Ltd.)

13

THE ORIGINS of enamelling on metal are vague as an art form but the history of this subject dates back at least 3000 years. The technique is basically one of fusing powdered glass to metal, either precious metals, such as gold and silver, or base metals, such as copper and bronze. This method of creating decorative objects has taken various forms throughout history.

CLOISONNE

This is a technique in which thin strips of metal are attached at right angles to a metal base to form small cells or compartments (*cloisons*) which contain the enamel. The cells are filled with a finely powdered glass paste which, after being fired in a furnace, fuses to the metal. On melting, the enamel shrinks and, when cool, the surface is depressed. More enamel is inserted and the process is repeated. Finally the surface is levelled by polishing.

Six Mycenaean gold rings discovered in a thirteenth century B.C. tomb at Kouklia, Cyprus, might be the earliest known examples of *cloisonné*, were it certain that these were made from powdered glass fused to metal and not merely by inserting fragments of coloured glass and fusing them by refiring, which would amount to a stage between inlay and enamelling. They appear to be a primitive form of *cloisonné*. Nearer to true *cloisonné* enamelling are later Mycenaean examples dating from approximately 100 B.C. It is possible that the art was passed on to the Greeks who introduced it to the Italians who in turn were responsible for spreading it throughout Europe. *Cloisonné* enamel was used to a minor degree on Greek gold jewellery, but was more extensively applied to Celtic metal-work by means of the process being applied to bronze objects. Byzantine enamelling, using the *cloisonné* method, began in about the late ninth century in Constantinople and reached great artistic heights in the eleventh century. The majority of Byzantine enamelled objects were on a base of finely beaten gold; were it not for this fact, a greater number of examples would have survived. Invaders from many countries carried off precious enamels, to be melted down for their gold content. The use of the *cloisonné* technique also appeared in Russia in the tenth century.

Chinese *cloisonné* was a later development. Although it was thought to have been in use from about the fourteenth century, the earliest objects of this type to be identified so far date from the early fifteenth century. A group from the reign of

Hsüan-tê (1426–36) of the Ming dynasty comprises bronze vessels decorated with turquoise blue, red, a lapis lazuli tinged with purple, yellow and white enamel within bronze *cloisons*. By the end of the fifteenth century, pale green and a semi-transparent purple known as Ming pink were introduced. Chinese *cloisonné* was at its peak during the eighteenth century but since that period it has declined in every way. Today it is still, however, a vast industry thriving on the manufacture of debased eighteenth-century designs. In Japan, *cloisonné* is believed to have arrived during the early seventeenth century. It was at first used principally to embellish sword attachments. Following a period in decline, in the 1830s the art of making *cloisonné* enamels was revived and new methods of 'rain-bowing' colours were devised. Towards the mid-nineteenth century, overcrowded Japanese floral designs were very popular with Western collectors. By the closing years of the nineteenth century, a new school flourished in Japan, in Kyoto, where precision wares were made using all manner of naturalistic themes and a wide palette of colours in *cloisonné* so fine that it gave the appearance of painted enamels.

CHAMPLEVE

This technique involves excavating the metal by cutting, hammering or gouging it in order to create depressions which will receive the powdered glass. The article is then fired, the glass is liquified and, on cooling, it fuses to the metal. The

Below: A reliquary casket of *champlevé* enamel on copper made at Limoges about 1180–1190. Scenes from the Martyrdom of St Valerie are set against a background decorated with vine-scroll motifs in the *vermiculé* manner. St Valerie was the patron of the city of Limoges and, according to legend, she was put to death following her refusal to marry the pro-consul Junius Silvanus who had succeeded her father as one of the Roman Governors of Aquitane. Width 5.2 cm (2 ins) (British Museum)

Right: An Italian gold and rock crystal miniature casket, the top and sides set with plaques engraved with figures copied from the three Predella panels from Raphael's painting of the Entombment of Christ in the Vatican; the interior of the base is set with a lapis lazuli plaque and the bottom is *champlevé* enamelled. The cast and chased male terms at each corner are enamelled *en ronde bosse*. Mid-sixteenth century. 8.7 cm (3½ ins) wide. A casket in the Geistliche Schatzkammer in Vienna was discovered to be an almost identical copy of this authentic example. The duplicate had been made by the notorious master faker, Salomon Weininger, who is mentioned on page 107. (Wartski, London)

first *champlevé* enamels to be identified with any certainty are Celtic of the Roman period. This process was employed not only by the Celts and Romans but was the chief method used by medieval enamellers from the close of the eleventh to the fourteenth century. In twelfth-century France, *champlevé* was widely practised in Limoges and in the valleys of the Rhine and the Meuse. The Rhenish and Mosan enamels are distinguished by the predominance of greens, yellows and blues which are of a lighter shade than those used at Limoges. In western Europe great developments were made in the *champlevé* technique and one of the finest examples of this period is the Klosterneuberg Altarpiece which was produced in 1181 by a supreme artist of the craft, Nicholas of Verdun.

Medieval craftsmen created an enriched form of *champlevé* decoration by backing their enamels with *paillons* or foils of metal. Warm shades of colour were produced by using a gold backing and cool shades by a silver one which reflected through the translucent enamels and thereby enhanced the colours.

In China, *champlevé* was used throughout the Ming dynasty (1368–1644) and was particularly encouraged during the reign of K'ang-Hsi (1662–1722). In oriental enamels, both *champlevé* and *cloisonné* were occasionally used in the same piece, the former for the bolder elements of a design, the latter for the finer. Examples of this combination of methods can also be found in early German pieces. *Champlevé* was also employed in Persia and India from at least as early as the seventeenth century.

ENCRUSTED or ENAMELS IN THE ROUND

A highly-skilled technique, first used by the Greeks and the Etruscans for jewellery, this was a method by which enamel was applied to figures in high relief or to fully sculptured detail. This form of enamelling was much practised on European jewellery of the Renaissance and also on larger scale works such as reliquaries and shrines.

During the Renaissance, a period of magnificence in the applied arts, jewellers, goldsmiths, lapidaries, engravers and enamellers combined to create wonderful jewels and vessels of rock crystal and coloured hardstone, with enamelled mounts. Antwerp and Milan were the principal centres of manufacture but craftsmen in Prague, Paris, Florence and Augsburg also participated in this rebirth of superlative skills. The technique is also referred to as *émail en ronde bosse*.

BASE TAILLE

A technique of enamelling in low-relief sculpture related to *champlevé*, *basse taille* was introduced towards the close of the

Far left: A gold miniature or photograph frame by Carl Fabergé. The body is decorated with apricot translucent enamel over a wavy *guillocage* with floral swags and bows painted in sepia; the entire frame is defined with green gold foliage borders and the corners are applied with red gold rosettes. The aperture is bordered with seed pearls and the gold scrolled strut is applied to an ivory back. Made *circa* 1900, it is signed 'Fabergé' and bears the initials of the chief workmaster, Henrik Wigstrom. Height 8 cm (3¼ ins) (Wartski, London)
Left: A delightful example of *basse-taille* enamelling on a small oval gold snuff-box. Exotic birds, flowers and foliage are enamelled in brilliant red, yellow, blue and green, against a chased all-over zig-zag diapered background. Made by Henri Delobel in Paris in 1752. Width 5.7 cm (2¼ ins) (Wartski, London)

17

thirteenth century and has been practised extensively in many parts of western Europe from this time. A metal surface is routed away, carved, hand engraved or worked in intaglio into a design. It is then covered with translucent enamel, thus creating a sense of sculptural modelling, achieved from the shading created by the varying depths of the enamel. The metal base, usually silver or gold, gives added brilliance to the applied enamel colours.

ENGINE-TURNED SURFACES

From the mid-eighteenth century a new technique was employed to decorate snuff-boxes and other small precious objects which enabled a wonderful variety of intricate designs to be achieved. This was made possible by the *tour à guillocher*, which effected an engine-turned (*guilloché*) ground; over this layers of translucent enamels could be applied, creating shimmering, richly-coloured surfaces.

Around 1900 the workshops of Carl Fabergé created unparalleled fantasies in enamel, employing various techniques including enamelling on a *guilloché* background. For many, the very word enamel evokes a special vision of luxury and magic due to his unique inventions. Kenneth Snowman's description in his book on Fabergé could not be bettered:

> 'Enamelling is not a cut-and-dried process learned as one learns how to assemble a wireless set: it is rather an empirical affair of the emotions and instincts, requiring a marvellous combination of the gardener's green fingers, and the touch of a successful pastry-cook to bring off a perfect job.'[1]

PLIQUE-A-JOUR

This development of *cloisonné* was an enamelling technique used in the fourteenth century and again during the nineteenth century. It was a method which created the effect of miniature stained glass windows by allowing light to shine through the translucent enamel. *Cloisons* of enamel were built up with the aid of a plate or backing which was removed afterwards. During the nineteenth century *plique-à-jour* enamelled spoons, cups, bowls and dishes were made in Norway, Sweden, France and Russia. Much Art Nouveau jewellery was made in this way by great French artists such as René Lalique, Henri Vever and Georges Fouquet, the technique being so well suited to the gossamer-like effects

which many of their designs demanded. Also, at the turn of
the nineteenth century, large articles made entirely by the
plique-à-jour method to create a totally translucent body were
produced in Japan.

EN PLEIN

En plein enamelling is decoration on comparatively large
surfaces or fields. The enamel 'floats' on the surface of the
gold, creating a layer of its own, rather than filling prepared recesses. This technique, which is exceedingly difficult
to accomplish, was popular in Paris from the mid-eighteenth
century, and was used occasionally from that time onwards in
Germany, in England, in Switzerland and, later, in Russia by
Fabergé.

PAINTED ENAMELS

It was perhaps natural that during the Renaissance enamellers should have wanted to express the human form using the
freedom which painting techniques provided. They knew
that, once they were able to control their colours and fluxes
and had mastered the temperatures at which each could be
fired without affecting the other colours, an enamel picture
could out-rival a painting in oils in its bid for permanence.

Right: An example of *en plein* enamelling on a highly decorative French eighteenth-century box. An oval chased *quatre couleur* gold snuff-box with scenes of cherubs enamelled *en grisaille* and reserved areas simulating pink marbling. The borders and pilasters have elaborate floral trails and coloured gold swags. It was made in Paris, probably by Germain Chaÿé, in 1784. Width 8.6 cm (3⅜ ins) (Wartski, London)

In Limoges, where the making of *champlevé* enamels had flourished from the eleventh to the fourteenth century, the sophisticated skills required to create painted enamels on metal were developed from about 1470. The earliest method employed produced white to grey tones on a very dark background, and was known as *en grisaille*; this was originally used to create cameo-type figures and portraits. Black or another very dark colour enamel was applied on the metal and fired. On to this ground opaque white enamel was painted and thinned in places to create shading, or grey shadows, achieved by the dark ground showing through. Later a limited palette of colours was introduced and gold leaf was used for additional embellishment.

In medieval times, it was customary for entire families to be devoted to a certain craft. One family would compete with another, the pride and honour in their collective achievement being of greater importance than individual skill. The names of the most famous Limoges families were Penicaud, Limousin, Nouaillier, Reymond, Courtey, Court and Laudin. Around 1530, it became customary for signatures or punched marks on the reverse of some enamel pictures to be covered with transparent *contre-émail* (enamel backing) so that the authorship could be revealed. During the fifteenth century, painted enamels were also produced in Italy and in Spain, but until about 1600 Limoges was the dominant centre for the art.

The technical problems of painting in polychromatic enamel colours were slowly overcome towards the end of the fifteenth century, great improvements in technique were made in the sixteenth century, and by the seventeenth century painting in full colour directly on to a metal base was widely practised.

In China, foreign, probably French, missionaries had taken the technique of painted enamels to Canton and to Peking at the end of the seventeenth century. Around 1713, Emperor K'ang-Hsi set up a workshop in Peking for the manufacture of enamels. Those from Canton are frequently decorated in the *famille rose* style, in which opaque rose pink predominates and this style flourished during the Ch'ien Lung period (1736–96). Examples can be found in which medallions of painted enamel are surrounded by a background composed of *cloisonné* work. By the turn of the eighteenth century, Canton enamels had deteriorated in colour and design. They were still being made in large quantities throughout the nineteenth century at Hoihow in Hainan, often on a silver base.

Left: A Limoges enamel ewer, painted *en grisaille* by Jean de Court, signed I. C. The decoration on the body shows Moses stretching his hand over the Red Sea and causing the waters to swallow up the army of Pharaoh on the other side; the Israelites are on dry land. On the shoulders, heightened with flesh tones, are Neptune and Amphitrite in the waves, surrounded by sea monsters. Height 28 cm (11 ins). Sixteenth century. (From the Collection of the Earls of Rosebery at Mentmore, by courtesy of Sotheby, Parke Bernet & Co.)

Right: A Chinese eighteenth-century Canton enamel tray, made for the European market. The shape is a copy of a European silver tray and the decoration is painted in the Chinese manner with flowers and fruit, using the *famille rose* palette of colours. The technique of painting enamels on a copper base was developed by Jesuit missionaries in China from around 1700 and was practised by Chinese craftsmen whom they trained. 76.3 cm (30½ ins) (John Sparks)

Around the second decade of the seventeenth century in France, Jean Toutin, a jeweller from Châteaudun with his son, Henri, and the enamellers of the Blois school, as well as artist-enamellers working in Geneva, began to create fine, small objects by using gold as a base and painting in colours on a white enamel ground. This method of painting was imitated by the watchmakers of France and other countries and can be seen at its best in the works of Petitot and Bordier (both pupils of the Toutins), Boit and his pupil, Zincke, Liotard, and other fine miniaturists. Petitot came from Paris to England in about 1637 and it was he who introduced to Britain the art of painting miniature portraits in enamel.

ENAMELLING IN ENGLAND

There are various enamelled objects which are thought to have been made in England before the art of painting with enamels was introduced there in the seventeenth century by French artist-craftsmen. Excavations in many places in the British Isles have resulted in Roman and Celtic enamelled horse trappings being discovered which are considered to date from the first century. Bronze hanging bowls decorated with *champlevé* enamel were discovered in the Sutton Hoo ship burial when it was excavated in 1939. These are thought to date from A.D. 625–630 and it is not certain whether they are Saxon or Celtic. A famous example of an early enamel is the Alfred Jewel which is in the Ashmolean Museum in Oxford; this was made in the ninth century by a method akin to *cloisonné*. *Basse taille* mitres, croziers, small medallions and shields have survived from the fourteenth and fifteenth centuries. In the seventeenth century, between 1650 and

1684, enamelled firedog's, candlesticks, vases and heraldic medallions were produced by a technique similar to *champlevé*. These were the so-called Surrey or Stuart enamels which are believed to have been made at the brass mills at Esher. The method was to cast the model in brass with a surface pattern in low relief, which was often engraved to improve the sharpness of the design; the recesses were then filled with enamel. A distinct Venetian influence is evident in the designs and it is thought probable that both the enamel and the craftsmen who used it originated in Venice.

In the latter part of the seventeenth century, a clockmaker, Nicholas Paris of Warwick, only 32 kilometres (20 miles) south-east of Birmingham, was famed for his *champlevé* enamelling; he died in 1716 but the workshop was carried on by his son, Thomas, who died in 1753.

It is perhaps surprising that copper-based painted enamel objects did not begin to be made in England on a really commercial scale until the late 1740s. Painted enamel on copper dials for watches had been widely produced from the early 1700s; what a comparatively small step it would have been then from the convex enamel dial, mounted into a hinged bezel, to the snuff-box or patch-box. But it took the influence of painted enamels from the Continent, coupled with the impetus of mid-eighteenth century fashion, to bring about the transition.

Boxes and so-called toys enamelled on copper were not well received at first. Early writers on the arts did not refer to them at all and those who were aware of their existence compared them unfavourably with gold-based enamels. 'For copper, beside that it emits a fume which tarnishes the colours, is apt to scale and crackle.'[2] But as the 1740s progressed they became accepted first as novelties and later they

Two English painted enamels. Below left: A box which was probably made to celebrate George III becoming Prince of Wales on the death of his father, Prince Frederick Louis, in 1751. On the lid a phoenix rises from the ashes and in the corners there are crowns and Prince of Wales feathers. Probably of London origin.
Below right: This box is thought to portray Bonnie Prince Charlie (1720–88) and Flora Macdonald, seen curtseying. For aiding the Prince's escape to the Hebrides she was imprisoned in the Tower of London. The box might have been made in London or in Birmingham on her release in 1747. Length 6.3 cm (2½ ins) (Eric Benton Collection)

were esteemed for their wit and charm. Until that time, few of the miniaturists, many of them of French and Swiss origin, who were working in England, principally in London, painted in enamels. The brilliance and durability of the medium, however, became increasingly appreciated and many of the country's finest artists were soon attracted to its use. In the metropolis and in the Midlands there were enamellers on metal, on glass, on china and there were also japanners. Many artists decorated several different materials; as 'Painters brought up in the Snuff-Box Way' they were adaptable.[3]

The early days of painted enamels in England are sparsely recorded. An advertisement in the *London Daily Advertiser*, 20 March 1747 reads:

'To be sold by auction . . . at Geare's Public Sale-Warehouse in Threadneedle Street behind the Royal Exchange . . . the effects of an enameller deceased consisting of watches, rings and snuff boxes, painted and blank plates, some colours, etc.'[4]

On 28 September 1747 *Aris's Birmingham Gazette* announced:

'This is to aquaint the curious, that a neat piece of shell or grotto work, enclosed in a Japan case, is to be disposed of by way of a raffle to fifty subscribers, at two shillings each, to be thrown for three dice and the next number to the prize to be entitled to an enamelled snuff box, value one pound.'[5]

Also in 1747, *A General Description of all Trades* records that:

'Enamelling is a curious art, and not much labour but that of laying and painting colours, plain or in figures, on metal. The masters in this way are not many; but they will take an apprentice £10 . . . Their hours of business are from six in the morning to eight at night; in which time a good hand will get three or four shillings, and a person may set up for himself with a little money.'[6]

In 1758, Robert Dossie in his *Handmaid to the Arts* referred to the enamellers of Geneva as already long experienced 'in this branch of commerce which gave them originally the greatest advantage in it over us.'[7]

There is a short petition for patent rights concerning enamel colours dated 2 July 1760 by 'Isaac Nerbell of the parish of St John, Southwark, in the county of Surrey, manufacturer of china ware'. Nerbell describes himself as a native of the canton of Bern in Switzerland, 'but hath been resident in England for twelve years past where he now resides with his family and intends solely to practise his said invention.' He states that:

> 'he has found out and invented a method of making enamel equal in goodness to the Venetian enamel (being the only enamel now used in England) from materials solely the produce of Great Britain.'[8]

But in 1765, the Society of Arts offered two prizes of £50 each in an attempt to improve home production of raw materials for the enamelling industry. One was offered to any person in England or Wales:

> 'who shall make the best white enamel, the same being equal in colour, and all other properties to the Venetian.'

The other prize was offered to:

> 'the person who shall make the finest true Red colour for the use of Enamel painters . . . No regard will be had to any that verges at all towards the purple.'[9]

When comparing the development of English enamels with the history of English porcelain and pottery, it is interesting to note how few manufacturers of the latter attempted to make mounted, hinged-lid boxes, even though the principal inspiration for English enamel boxes came from those made in porcelain on the Continent. Beginning with the superb products of Nicholas Sprimont's Chelsea factory in the 1750s, many manufacturers made elaborately decorated porcelain and pottery which could so easily have been formed into box-shapes using the mounts which were then readily available; of the few who did, only Chelsea achieved fame for the exquisite *bibelots* made there.

Porcelain and pottery boxes with 'lift-off' lids were manufactured in innumerable forms, but apart from Thomas Whieldon's agate-ware boxes in the 1740s, a minimal production of snuff-boxes made by Wedgwood in the 1770s, and toys and *bonbonnières* made at Chelsea, none of them were mounted and hinged.

English enamel designs were based on objects made of precious metals, on the works of the Continental porcelain factories which included Meissen, Nymphenberg, Mennecy, St Cloud and Sèvres, as well as on the porcelain toys made at Chelsea. The *tabatières* and *bonbonnières* in animal, fruit and human forms from those factories were the models for the small embossed and painted enamel toys. The shapes and decoration of English enamel snuff-boxes, *étuis*, tea caddies, inkwells and other objects were inspired by similar examples from the same sources. It seems incredible that manufacturers in the Staffordshire potteries did not take advantage of the abundance of metal mounts which were being made in the Birmingham and Wolverhampton areas, within easy reach of their factories, to create porcelain boxes such as their contemporaries across the Channel were making. It can only be assumed that in England the success of the enamellers

Right: Bilston enamel toys took many forms and embossed *bonbonnières* in animal shapes were extremely popular. The original inspiration for these was similar objects made in porcelain at Meissen and at Chelsea. These three fine examples date from about 1770, but cheaper versions were later produced. The pug dog's head measures 5 cm (2 ins) in diameter. (Halcyon Days)

was at first so great that it would not have been worthwhile for porcelain manufacturers to compete; and later on, due to the decline in snuff-taking, the vogue for the painted or transfer-printed box had passed.

In 1968, when the twentieth-century revival of English enamels was beginning in Bilston, the greatest obstacle to be overcome was the difficulty in obtaining hinged mounts in base metal in sufficient numbers to allow an enamelling factory to get into production. Jewellers could be found who would manufacture small lots, at high prices, but it transpired that this by-product of the silversmith, a hinged metal mount, made to be attached to a base and lid composed of a different material, had not been produced in quantity since the decline of the English enamel trade early in the nineteenth century.

Although production of eighteenth-century types of boxes and *bibelots* had ceased by the 1840s, other styles of enamelling gained in popularity. The Great Exhibition of 1851 gave a great impetus to designers and manufacturers. The British firm of Elkington made elaborate household articles embellished with enamel, the prototypes for these having been commissioned from French craftsmen. This had the not unexpected result of encouraging the French to compete in this field and the Parisian bronze foundry Barbedienne did so with considerable success, ornamenting their wares with *champlevé* and *cloisonné* enamelling. These found a ready market in England. The English were among the principal patrons of the French revival of Limoges enamels which had started at Sèvres in the 1840s. Because of this interest in England, the French enameller Adrien-Louis Dalpayrat went over to teach at the South Kensington Museum in London, and inspired many artists to create painted enamels. One of these was Alexander Fisher whose work, which was in the manner of the Renaissance enamellers, enjoyed a considerable success from the 1880s onwards. About this time, a Roman family of jewellers, Carlo Giuliano and his sons, Frederico and Fernando, established shops in London. They created elaborate designs for small luxury articles as well as jewels, using enamelling techniques which dated back to ancient times.

The Arts and Crafts movement encouraged a proliferation of painted enamels; artists such as Phoebe Traquair, and Kate M. Eadie as well as the workshops of Omar Ramsden and others whose works were sponsored by the firm of Liberty of London produced fine enamels during the Art Nouveau period, but by the 1920s the vogue had passed.

From the third quarter of the nineteenth century until recent times in England, as well as on the Continent, enamelled silver—and less frequently gold– dressing-table sets, photograph frames, coffee spoons, cigarette cases, watches and other personal accessories have been mass-produced on a vast scale. Translucent enamelling on an engine-turned ground, sometimes incorporating painted flowers or motifs, was the technique employed for this type of commercial product.

The early painted enamels produced on the Continent were the forerunners of the eighteenth-century English snuffboxes and curiosities produced in London, Birmingham, South Staffordshire and Liverpool. It was these objects which were made to delight those of taste and discernment in the eighteenth century and which continue to give pleasure to this day. The successful revival of the craft in the twentieth century has brought the charm of English enamels to an even wider public.

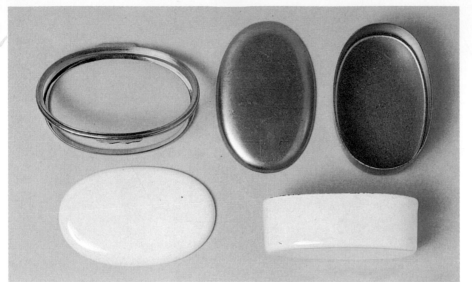

1. The copper components of an enamel box showing the gilt-brass hinged mounts and the lid and base before and after their initial white enamel coating.

2. Components from the Halcyon Days Enamels box illustrated on the facing page, showing the charcoal outline transfer after firing and the fully hand-painted lid and base, before being assembled.

3. Using a modern alternative technique, the components of a box produced by Halcyon Days Enamels in association with the Wallace Collection, London, show the initial part-colour transfer and the completed overpainted lid and base. The design is after an 18th-century Sèvres porcelain plaque.

Manufacturing Processes

Enamelling is an ancient and fascinating craft and also one of the most difficult to accomplish. Patience and great skill are required to achieve successful results.

Enamelling on copper involves many stages. The basic ingredients are combined to form enamel powder and the metal components are shaped. Today's methods are akin to those used in the 18th-century but, in addition to taking advantage of modern technology, they avoid outdated processes that endangered the health of Georgian craftsmen. The copper parts are no longer laboriously hammered by hand but are pressed by machine; they are then annealed, cleansed and etched with acid to roughen the surface and give a firm hold to the enamel, several layers of which are applied, each individually fired in electric kilns – not in the smoke-emitting furnaces of centuries past. Designs are applied by transferring ceramic lithographs that replace the 18th-century engraved copper-plate technique. As shown opposite, the transfer can be a single colour outline (2) to guide hand painting or it can be part-coloured (3) transferring two or more colours on to the subject as preparation for the final painting by hand. At each stage the enamel parts are fired at around 800°C and they can receive many firings before a picture is finally completed.

Above: Scenes of Vauxhall Gardens—the London playground for Georgian society—decorate this box with a romantic theme. An orchestra is seen playing in one of the galleries as a fashionable public saunters by. The lovers in the foreground prompted the quotation from Shelley: 'Are we not formed as notes of music are. For one another, though dissimilar,' which is inscribed inside the base. The drawings on this limited edition box are by Moira Hoddell. Length 7.3 cm (2 ins) (Halcyon Days)

A BASIC CORE of copper was common to all the English painted and printed enamels discussed in this book. In the eighteenth century, most of the copper used for enamelling was obtained from the Ecton Hill Copper Mine in Staffordshire. In 1769 more than 300 men, women and children were employed there, working a 72-hour week. The top wage was twopence an hour and boys and girls on haulage and sorting jobs might earn no more than twopence a day.

The copper was beaten or drawn through steel rollers until it was paper thin, softened by annealing (heating and gradual cooling), and then cut into a blank, preparatory to being hammered, spun, jointed or stamped into the required shape. The technique of stamping metal was invented in 1769 by Richard Ford, a Birmingham toy-maker. Prior to this invention, rounded shapes were achieved in one of two ways: either the malleable, thin copper blank was placed over a convex form of the required shape and then struck with a similarly shaped but concave, hard-wood mallet, or the blank was spun by being rotated over a hard-wood chuck of the required shape, to form a circular hollow shape. Rectangular and other deep shapes were jointed, the edges being placed together, overlapped and folded.

Scent bottles and elaborately embossed articles, formed as animals, fruit, or other natural shapes, were originally made in sections. These were beaten into the required shapes by the *repoussé* method and joined together by overlapping or lacing. When they were laced, the edges were punched or drilled with tiny holes and very fine copper wire was used to assemble the parts; the seams were finally flattened by hammering. All of the above methods were made possible by the fact that repeated annealing and hammering renders copper as malleable and thin as tin foil. In almost every instance, the joins were indiscernible when covered both sides with enamel. In the 1790s the introduction of long-wearing cast steel enabled multiple-sectioned steel dies to be made for the stamping, often in one piece, of intricately shaped hollow forms. This resulted in increased production of a variety of cheaper boxes shaped as whole animals and birds.

Further annealing was required after the shape was formed —this removed stresses from the copper and reduced distortion during the firing of the enamel. The copper article was then cleansed by being plunged into diluted nitric acid for several minutes, washed, and the surfaces finally roughened with a stiff brass brush to give a firm hold for the enamel.

The copper shell was now ready for enamelling. Enamel was made in two separate stages, the first being to produce a raw state of enamel glass called 'frit'. This was a mixture of washed flint glass and/or lead crystal (much use was made of broken glasses from pubs) mixed with potassium carbonate, borax, feldspar, quartz, oxides of tin and other inorganic materials. These were smelted together for several hours in a brick-lined furnace at temperatures between 1100°C (2045°F) and 1300°C (2435°F) and occasionally raked until a consistent molten state had been achieved. The molten glass was then quenched by being tipped or ladled into cold water to produce frit, which had the appearance of shattered glass. By varying the basic frit formulae transparent or translucent enamels known as 'flux' were produced. Opaque enamels were made by smelting frit with tin oxide. Semi-opaque or opalescent enamels were made by mixing together transparent and opaque enamels.

The second stage involved grinding the enamel in a mill for many hours until a talcum powder-like fineness was achieved. The majority of coloured enamels for backgrounds, transfer-printing and hand decorating were made by the introduction of mineral oxides into flux by one of two methods: either by taking a measure of the unground flux and re-smelting it together with the oxide to form a coloured glass, prior to being ground, or by adding colouring oxide to the mill and grinding it together with the flux. If only small quantities were required these were ground with a pestle and mortar.

The next procedure was to cleanse thoroughly the enamel powder by immersing it many times in clear water, then in nitric acid (to dissolve any metal particles gathered during grinding) and finally to rinse it repeatedly in water until all traces of the acid were removed.

The enamel powder was then dried and sifted through a fine hair sieve, mixed with a volatile oil such as oil of sassafras or spike (lavender) oil and applied to the surface of the copper by brush or palette knife, to form a groundcoat. Several additional layers were necessary to build up the required thickness before decorating could take place. The enamel object had to be fired between each coat at temperatures which varied between 750°C (1415°F) and 850°C (1625°F). Both inside and outside surfaces were coated with the same thickness of enamel which helped to overcome the problem of warping caused by the rapid expansion of the copper during firing. With the introduction of cheaper white enamel, the chief ingredients of which were powdered flint glass and arsenic, enamels were coated by being dipped into 'slurry', which is composed of enamel powder mixed with water and with clay.

Firing took place in a small iron kiln or furnace containing a muffle, heated with pit-coal. Until about 1780, when larger kilns were introduced, the largest article which could be fired measured approximately 20 centimetres (eight inches) across. Prior to 1780, tall candlesticks were made in sections which were joined together with gilt metal mounts. The articles to be fired were put in clay coffins or saggers, boxes which measured 25 by 16 by (depth) 18 centimetres (10 by 6 by 7 inches) with, when small articles were fired, a second layer on a wrought iron tray supported on 8 centimetre (3 inch) columns; the base of the coffin and the tray were thickly coated with chalk to prevent the contents from sticking; the coffin or sagger was sealed with fire-lute (a tenacious clay) to prevent smoke or fumes from entering. To test the furnace, a piece of tile coated with the same enamel was put on top of the coffin before it was placed in the kiln. The enameller, who wore a cloth helmet with a tinted glass aperture to protect his face and eyes from the intense, bright white heat could see the test tile through a small peephole in the kiln door. There was a Bilston legend that these weird creatures, operating at night, their masked faces reflecting flickering red flames, were the devil's accomplices. The coffin was first warmed on the top of the kiln and then carefully placed inside. When the firing was completed it was removed with a flat iron shovel and put on top of the kiln to cool gradually before it was opened and the fired enamels were taken out. Rapid cooling would have resulted in brittle enamel, which would easily have cracked or scaled.

Once the satisfactory background enamel had been achieved, the articles were ready for decorating by transfer-printing, painting, gilding or a combination of two or all of these methods. Mineral colours were used, as vegetable colours would have disappeared during firing. The mineral colours, for example oxide of cobalt for blue, carbonate of copper for green, oxide of manganese for violet, were mixed with the flux, the various mixtures giving fluxes that would fire at different temperatures as was necessary. As enamel colours matured at varying temperatures, those requiring the highest firing were applied first, and so on. It was not unusual for a picture to receive as many as six or more firings for this reason. Extreme care had to be taken each time to prevent colours being over-fired, thereby damaging beyond repair a piece on which much time had been spent. Also, most enamel colours change completely during firing, making it essential for the enamel painter to anticipate the inevitable transformation. Preparatory to hand painting, a small amount of the

coloured flux was re-ground with spike oil, and then mixed on a china tile together with turpentine which had been left uncorked until it had thickened and had become 'fatty'. The colour was then ready for painting in the normal way with a sable brush. The highly volatile spike oil was allowed to evaporate partly, leaving the article ready for firing when all traces of the oil would burn away.

Transfers were produced by taking impressions from an engraved copper plate. The special enamel ink was rubbed into the incised lines of a warmed copper plate, which was then polished, leaving the ink only in the finely engraved grooves and recesses of the design which, contrary to one intended for an engraving or book illustration, was not reversed. A sheet of gummed paper was then put on the still warm plate and covered with a double thickness of flannel. This 'sandwich' was then rolled through a press under considerable pressure. The plate, with the paper, was then heated, causing the enamel ink, now formed as minute ridges of colour, to adhere firmly to the paper which lifted from the plate. The enamel was smeared with linseed oil and the dampened printed paper was placed on to it and rubbed all over so that there was complete contact without any air bubbles; it was then fired in a kiln causing the ink to combine with the enamel and the paper to burn away. This was an unreliable method as impurities in the paper could result in blemishes which were revealed only after firing. These were occasionally obscured by over-painting and re-firing.

An alternative procedure was to cover the area to be decorated with an amber, varnish-like 'size', which remained tacky. The paper bearing the design was placed on to the sized area, pressure was exerted by rubbing all over the back of the paper, and then either the paper was sponged off with soapy water or the article was immersed in water, at which point the paper would lift off, leaving the design adhered to the tacky area. On firing, the size burnt away and the design fused into the surface of the enamel. Procedures varied in different workshops, each enameller developing his own formulae and methods.

In many instances transfer prints were so expertly over-painted that the outline of the transfer was almost imperceptible. This was not necessarily done to deceive; it was quite simply making the most of available techniques.

Another transfer-printing process called bat-printing (also known as black-printing, even when carried out in other colours) was sometimes used. This method was devised as a means of recreating on ceramic surfaces (enamels included) the delicacy and subtlety of the chalk, stipple or dotted manner of engraving for prints. The method was said to have been introduced into England about 1760–61 by William Wynne Ryland, on his return from study in France. Ryland was thought to have been one of the artists at the Battersea factory. He was a pupil of Battersea's most famous engraver, Ravenet, and was eventually appointed engraver to George III. In 1783 he met a tragic end, not unrelated to his expertise. He was the last man to be hanged at Tyburn, having been found guilty of forging a bank note in an attempt to retrieve his dissipated fortunes.

In bat-printing, a bat consisting of a sheet of glue about three millimetres (one-eighth inch) thick was used, instead of gummed paper. A finely stippled copper plate in the style of a Bartolozzi print was used instead of a line engraving, the strength of colour varying with the closeness and the size of the dots. First the design was filled with linseed oil instead of ink, then, after being pressed by hand against the copper plate, the bat was pressed on to the glazed enamel surface and lifted, leaving an impression in oil of the design. This was then pounced or dusted with powdered enamel colour, when as if by magic (the pattern in oil being all but in-visible unless held against the light) the design materialized. It was then fired in the usual way.

It is possible that the rare gold transfers of Battersea were produced by a similar method, the sticky oil impression probably being transferred via special paper rather than by a glue bat and, after the removal of the paper, gold enamel powder was dusted on to the design prior to firing. The early gold decoration at other factories, which was not permanent and only slight traces of which have survived, was produced by painting the design in gold size, pressing gold leaf on to it and then removing the superfluous gold with a soft brush. Another method was to grind the gold leaf to a fine powder, mix it with honey, spike oil or gum and water, paint the design with it and then fire it at a low temperature. This gilding had a slightly dull appearance but if applied thickly could be burnished with an agate or metal point. In about 1765 a cheaper method of mercury-gilding was introduced, an amalgam of finely powdered gold and an equal quantity of mercuric oxide being used. This method produced permanent gilding, but so strong were the fumes emitted during the firing that workers ran a considerable risk of slow death from mercury poisoning.

The resulting gold decoration was very dull, required burnishing, and having a somewhat brassy appearance did not compare with the previous method. The gilded rococo scrollwork frames surrounding painted reserves which frequently appeared on the finest, most elaborately decorated English enamels, were produced by the application of a thick enamel paste which was fired, painted with a gold layer and re-fired.

A transparent glaze which completely covered the finished, decorated enamel was occasionally applied. This gave an effect of depth to the decoration and also protected finely printed areas from deterioration; a scratch which would badly damage an unglazed print would be barely perceptible on the glaze. A large proportion of Battersea enamels were over-glazed and this protective coating can occasionally be seen even on small patch-boxes. A similar finish is found on enamels which have been so expertly repaired that the work of the restorer is imperceptible. This clear glaze is particularly obvious on enamels made from the late eighteenth century in Geneva. It created a thick, glass-like layer over painted enamels thereby minimizing the chipping of snuff-boxes, watches and other small articles in everyday use.

On close inspection flaws can sometimes be observed on

even the finest copper-based enamels: tiny pin holes, called pitting, a defect resulting from the application of too thick a layer of enamel; a bubbled effect where enamel has been applied thickly and fired before being allowed to dry out completely; hairline cracks running through the base coat, the result of firing the painting colours at too low a temperature; fading and speckling caused by over-firing; crazing on flat areas—at once apparent, where it might not be on uneven surfaces. Enamelling on copper is, inevitably, an imprecise craft. Minor impurities in the metal might not manifest themselves until the last of many firings. When small articles of base metal are coated with paper-thin vitreous enamel and then subjected to the white-hot heat of a furnace, the ensuing stresses invariably result in perceptible variations. Occasionally one can detect that an insect or a leaf has been painted in to hide a blemish.

It is these very imperfections which account, in part, for the charm of English painted and printed enamels. Objects which are manufactured by entirely predictable processes have a precision, a rigidity to their appearance, in which hazard plays no part. English enamels, at their best, have a certain softness, a 'sweet disorder', and are the more beguiling for it.

The final process of manufacture was mounting; plaques were mounted in chased gilt copper frames with baroque scrolls or *rocaille* ornaments or in thin bands of plain, tooled or punch-decorated metal. Some fine early boxes were mounted in gold or silver but the majority of mounts were made of gilt copper or other alloys.

Christopher Pinchbeck, a Fleet Street watch and clock-maker, gave his name to one of these alloys which he had developed with great success. This metal, pinchbeck, so closely resembled gold that in 1734, two years after its inventor's death, someone wrote of a despondent jeweller that 'the nobility and gentry run so much into Pinchbeck that he had not disposed of two gold watches this month'.[1]

The hinges which joined the metal rim mounts of the base and lid of the earlier boxes were made with great care and stretched the whole width of the box, having anything up to seven joints and being almost invisible. The rims, attached without any adhesive, were so perfectly fitted that even finely powdered snuff could not escape. The mounts of the boxes were frequently decorated by engraving, gadrooning (a raised, ridged pattern) or beading. On the inside edges of fine mounts, incised numerals can sometimes be observed.

In the late 1760s, the suage-block began to be used to

shape mounts. Thin strips of softer alloy were drawn through two steel blocks, the side of one cut concavely and the other convexly to the shape the strip was required to assume. The strip was then soldered on to a heavier flat strip, sometimes enclosing a wire core, thus producing a strong mount. The larger boxes, candlesticks and other sizeable articles often had mounts around the base and some important caskets also had strips of metal applied vertically to the side panels and corners. Early boxes of good quality also had base mounts to protect the lower edges. Scent bottles were mounted at the neck and had cast gilt metal stoppers with an ornamental finial attached to the mount by a small chain.

Around 1780, a cheaper and more efficient method of alloying copper and zinc was discovered by James Emerson of Bristol. At about the same time a method of decorating strips of brass for mounts, by rolling them between steel rollers on which the destined design had been cut, was invented by William Bell. These inventions were soon used by mount-makers, but while greatly reducing the cost of mounting they led to the cheap mass-production of boxes.

In the last quarter of the eighteenth century, mount-making had become a specialized craft in Birmingham, Bilston, Wednesbury and Wolverhampton, and in London, Benjamin Cartwright is reputed to have made mounts for Battersea. All aspects of metal-working were prolific in eighteenth-century London, and mounts would have been easily procured there from watchmakers and silversmiths. It is, however, possible that some of the box mounts, frames for plaques, and the basic copper forms for enamels made at Battersea and at other London workshops were of Midland manufacture.

Salt cellars, beakers, inkstands, trays, small sweetmeat and counter dishes were not mounted. Such objects were often decoratively pierced, and the edges were sometimes scalloped and sometimes chamfered (bevelled) and folded inwards; when they had been dipped in enamel and fired the extra thickness of the rim was barely visible.

Two important works of reference and instruction, both published in the mid-eighteenth century, were Diderot's massive *Encyclopédie ou Dictionnaire raisonné des sciences, des arts et des métiers* (published from 1751–65) and Dossie's *Handmaid to the Arts* (1758). While covering a wide range of processes in the arts in general, each dealt extensively with enamelling techniques and formulae and afforded both student and practised craftsman an invaluable guide to methods of production.

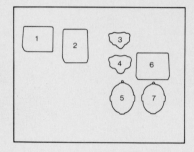

1 This box is a perfect example of a Battersea lid fitted to a Birmingham base of a later date, both transfer-printed in brown. On the lid is a print of Porsenna and Mucius Scaevola by Ravenet after the engraving by Jacob Schmutzel (1733–1811) from the painting by Paul Rubens (1577–1640). The interior lid bears a print of Apollo and Daphne, by Ravenet. The base is decorated with an engraving from a worn or re-engraved plate of the diaper and shell design used at Battersea. Length 8.5 cm (3⅜ ins) (Wolverhampton Museum)

2 A snuff-box with all of the features which today combine to form the generally accepted attribution 'Battersea'. Transfer-painted in puce, the lid bears an engraving of Britannia presenting a medal surrounded by the Arts and Sciences, after Ravenet and possibly after James Gwin; inside the lid is a profile portrait of Frederick Prince of Wales, and on the sides Ravenet's Children as Arts, Science and Commerce. The base shows boys with the British lion, flag and shield. Length 8.8 cm (3½ ins) (Halcyon Days)

3 CAPE, a Battersea bottle ticket of a cartouche shape, transfer-printed in red and painted with a blackamoor embracing a leopard. Width 6.3 cm (2½ ins) (Bernard Watney Collection)

4 BEER, a Battersea bottle ticket of a cartouche shape, transfer-printed in sepia and painted with two putti reaping the barley harvest. Width 6.3 cm (2½ ins) (Bernard Watney Collection)

5 Frederick Prince of Wales (1707–51) was the eldest son of George II and father of George III. The engraving on this oval medallion, transfer-printed in brownish-red, is by Ravenet, taken from a wax medallion by Isaac Gosset (1713–99) executed about 1749. Height 8.7 cm (3½ ins) (Wolverhampton Museum)

6 Venus mourning the death of Adonis. This oblong Battersea plaque is transfer-printed in grey with an engraving which was probably by Ravenet. This engraving is also found on other plaques. Width 10.2 cm (4⅛ ins) (Wolverhampton Museum)

7 The Magdalen, engraved by Ravenet; an oval Battersea medallion transfer-printed and painted in enamel colours. Height 8.7 cm (3½ ins) (Wolverhampton Museum)

York House, Battersea

Few names in the decorative arts have achieved lasting fame in so short a period as Battersea. In less than three years the enamels made there acquired a special reputation which has endured.

UNTIL THE publication of Bernard Rackham's catalogue of the Schreiber Collection at the Victoria and Albert Museum in 1924, which redirected research on the subject, practically all, certainly all the finest, English eighteenth-century painted and printed enamels on copper were believed to have been made at Battersea. Many collectors and even some less well-informed dealers still hold this belief.

In fact, almost the only enamels that can with any certainty be ascribed to the factory at York House, Battersea, which existed only from 1753 to 1756, consist of a group of plaques, snuff-boxes and labels (variously referred to as bottle tickets, wine and decanter labels) which were decorated with finely printed engravings and were occasionally delicately hand-coloured.

It was known that English copper-based enamels were first made in the 1740s and some, thought to have originated at Battersea, could be dated around 1750–51 on the grounds that their subject matter related to events in those years. Perhaps the most famous of these was a plaque inscribed 'Success to the British Fishery' which was long considered to be a prime example of a 'Battersea' enamel. This could be dated at approximately 1750, the Free British Fishery Society having been inaugurated on 25 October 1750 and the cause being one in which Stephen Theodore Janssen, who had inherited York House and who was the founder of the Battersea enterprise, played a leading part. But the approximate opening date of the manufactory was not known until 1931 when the late W. B. Honey, of the Victoria and Albert Museum, examined the rate books for the borough. There he discovered that no rates were collected on York House until the third quarter of 1753, the entries of the several preceding years recording that the property was 'empty'.

The factory at York House, formerly the London residence of the Archbishop of York, was started by a partnership of three, the name of the company being recorded as 'Messrs. Jansen (sic), Delamain & Brooks.' Stephen Theodore Janssen (son of Sir Thomas Janssen, a prominent city merchant who had become wealthy as a promoter of South Sea schemes) was the dominant partner and a public figure of some consequence. He was Sheriff of the City of London in 1749, Member of Parliament for London from 1747 to 1754, Master of the Worshipful Company of Stationers, Alderman of the Broad Street Ward, Vice President of the Free British Fishery Society, the Grand President of the Anti-Gallican Society, Lord Mayor in 1754, Chamberlain of London in

1765 and successor to the title of Baronet on the death of his brother in 1766. When he was returned for London as an opposition Whig in 1747, the Prime Minister, Henry Pelham, observed in a letter to Horace Walpole 'I could have wished the merchants had chosen a better subject than Janssen, but forward fellows fare best in this world.'[1]

Henry Delamain, the second partner, was an Irish potter who had introduced coal-firing to the Delftware industry and made the claim in 1753 that he had purchased 'the art of printing earthenware with as much beauty, strong impression and dispatch as can be done on paper.'[2] Delamain's interest in transfer-printing was for decorating earthenware—the 'Stove [a misspelling for Stone] Plates and Dutch Tiles' that were part of the stock at York House. (Stone Plates were stoneware pottery and decorated tiles were known as 'Dutch' at this period). The third partner, John Brooks, was an engraver from Dublin who had established a studio in the Strand in 1746. Brooks, a disreputable character, is accredited as the inventor of transfer-printing on 'Enamel, China, Glass, Delft and other Wares'.[3] He made unsuccessful petitions for a patent in 1751 from Birmingham and in 1754 and 1755 from Battersea. At this time the idea of transfer-printing was, so to speak, in the air, which is probably why Brooks' petitions met with failure. The process was being used for printing linen at a factory in County Meath, Ireland. Writing from Delville in December 1752, a Mrs Delany mentioned a visit:

> 'to Drumcondra, half a mile off, to see a new manu-
> factory that is set up there, of printed linen done by
> *copper-plates;* they are excessive pretty . . .'[4]

The conception of printing on to surfaces other than paper had been under consideration by others. Some 20 years later, in 1773, Benjamin Franklin wrote in a letter:

> 'I was much pleased with the specimens you so
> kindly sent me of your new art of engraving . . .
> I have reason to apprehend that I might have
> given the hint on which the improvement was
> made; for more than twenty years since, I wrote to
> Dr Mitchell from America, proposing to him the
> printing of square tiles for ornamenting chimneys,
> from copper plates . . .'[5]

Janssen presumably supplied the capital for the enterprise and, being a stationer, was doubtless able to obtain suitable

Above: Two fine transfer-printed Battersea plaques in their original gilt copper frames. The one on the left, in sepia, shows Paris presenting the apple to Hibernia in the presence of Britannia, after Ravenet and after an original by James Gwin. Height 9 cm (3¾ ins) (Halcyon Days). The plaque on the right, in purple, is a famous Ravenet engraving of the priest Laocoon and the Trojan Horse. This subject reflects the fashion in the mid-eighteenth century for the neoclassical movement, which gained in momentum as the century progressed.

paper for transferring the engravings. Transfer-printing was most likely the chief reason for setting up the concern; Brooks provided the expertise required to implement the process and Delamain's experience as a potter made him an ideal person to be in charge of the kilns.

There was trouble at York House within the first year. The rate book reveals that by the first quarter of 1754, only six months after the business started, Brooks had ceased to be a partner. By the third quarter of 1754, Delamain's name had also been removed, the occupier of York House appearing as 'Messrs. Jansen & Compy.' The entry for the last quarter of 1756 shows the premises as 'empty' once again.

Janssen was made bankrupt on 12 January 1756, but it would appear that production ceased long before then, making the life-span of actual manufacturing less than two years. An article in the *Anthologia Hibernica* of May 1793 dealing with the York House activities of Brooks (whose bankruptcy on 27 January 1756 was declared only 15 days after Janssen's) stated:

'This manufacture might have been very advantageous but through the bad management and dissipated conduct of Brooks it was in great measure the cause of the ruin of Janssen who was Lord Mayor of London at that time, but the Commission of Bankruptcy was withheld until his office was expired.'[6]

42

Janssen's term of office as Lord Mayor expired in November 1755.

It is recorded that his affairs later improved. After the bankruptcy he lived abroad for some years, but he had paid his debts in full, with interest, by the time he was elected Chamberlain of the City of London in 1765. He died at Wimbledon, aged 90, in 1777, leaving five sons and three daughters.

The enamel project probably failed through lack of direction following the departure of the two skilled partners. Janssen was an artistic aristocrat, living in style in a house in St Paul's Churchyard, a friend of the most eminent painters of the day, the patron of leading engravers and a man of wide-ranging interests. His many involvements possibly prevented him from saving the York House venture from collapse but it is not known whether this precipitated his personal financial disaster.

An advertisement relating not to York House but to his home appeared in the *Daily Advertiser* on 28 February 1756:

> 'To be sold by auction by Robert Heath, by order of the Assignees, on Thursday next and the following days, The genuine Household Furniture, Plate, Linen, China and Books, of Stephen Theodore Janssen, Esq., at his House in St Paul's Church-yard . . .
>
> Also a quantity of beautiful enamels, colour'd and uncolour'd of the new manufactory carried on at York House at Battersea, and never yet exhibited to public view, consisting of Snuff-boxes of all sizes of great variety of Patterns, of square & oval pictures of the Royal Family, History & other pleasing subjects, very proper ornaments for Cabinets of the Curious, Bottle Tickets with Chains for all sorts of Liquor, and of different Subjects, Watch-cases, Toothpick-cases, Coat & Sleeve Buttons, Crosses and other Curiosities, mostly mounted in metal, double gilt.'[7]

The listing of such miscellaneous articles as toothpick-cases and buttons is no proof that they were made at York House. It was then common practice for a manufacturer to increase his trade by buying in finished goods made by others. In his description of the green closet in the villa at Strawberry Hill, Horace Walpole mentions a 'kingfisher and ducks of the Battersea enamel: it was a manufacture stamped with a copper-plate, supported by Alderman Janssen, but failed.'[8] It is now considered that the kingfisher plaque was of Birmingham origin and that it might have been one of the items acquired by Janssen to supplement his stock.

Another advertisement appeared the following June, announcing the sale of the furniture, good-will and stock-in-trade at York House:

'To be sold by auction by order of the assignees on Monday next, June 8, 1756, and the following days, at York Place, at Battersea, in Surrey—
The household furniture and entire stock, of Stephen Theodore Janssen, Esq., consisting of a great Variety of beautiful enamelled Pictures, Snuff-Boxes, Watch-Cases, Bottle Tickets, Etc. great Variety of the like Enamels not completely finished, great Variety of Black [a misspelling for blank] Enamels of various Sizes, Copper-Frames for mounting of the unfinished Enamels, with all the Utensils, etc. belonging to the Manufactory; as also a great Number of Copper Plates beautifully engraved by the best Hands, some hundred Dozens of Stove Plates and Dutch Tiles, painted and plain, with many other Particulars, which will be specified in the printed Catalogue, which will be ready to be delivered at the House on Friday and Saturday next, the days of viewing, by T. Humphreys, Upholder, in St Paul's Churchyard, and by Mr Chesson, Upholder, in Fenchurch Street. The place is most pleasantly situated, with a convenient creek for barges and boats coming up to the house, which has been fitted up at very great expense, with every conveniency for carrying on the said manufactory, which if any person should think of continuing, they may be treated with by the assignees before the day of the sale.'[9]

Nobody did carry on 'the said manufactory' as it remained unoccupied after the end of June. Unfortunately no copy of the sale catalogue has been discovered. Other enamellers of London, Birmingham, South Staffordshire and Liverpool obviously took advantage of a rare opportunity to inspect and possibly to purchase a rival's equipment and stock. The dispersal of Battersea copper-plates and components has created many problems of similarity of design between objects made in different places—to the bewilderment of collectors of both enamels and contemporary porcelain. The 'great

Variety of Black [blank] Enamels' offered at the sale explains the occasional discovery of a Battersea lid on a box base enamelled elsewhere, and vice versa. To add to the confusion, Battersea engraved plates were used by other enamellers after the sale. And when the original plates were too worn to be used, the designs—so much were they esteemed—were copied by lesser engravers.

The engravers at York House included Brooks, few of whose engravings have been identified on enamels. There is a possibility that portraits of the famous Gunning sisters were produced during his pre-Battersea or Birmingham period. Another engraver, perhaps the most famous of all to be connected with enamels, was Simon François Ravenet, a Frenchman who had been an associate of J.P. le Bas and who came to England in 1744 at the invitation of Hogarth. Ravenet's engravings are technically the most brilliant and artistically

Left: A Battersea plaque, transfer-printed in red, after Hogarth's *Modern Midnight Conversation*, possibly engraved by Simon François Ravenet, the principal engraver at Battersea who came to England at Hogarth's invitation in 1744. Hogarth's engravings expressed his views which were that, prostitution apart, the greatest English vice of the eighteenth century was drunkenness. This plaque portrays a group of men around a table, on which there is a large bowl of punch. Width 11.7 cm (4⅝ ins) (Victoria & Albert Museum)

the most satisfying that have ever been used to decorate enamel. It is perversely fortunate that the York House factory had such a short life, for Ravenet's plates benefited by being used there only while still in pristine condition, thus being spared the deterioration which is the inevitable result of constant use.

His work includes an exquisite series to decorate decanter labels, in which *putti* (cherubs) are engaged in work connected with the name on the label. These same engravings have also been found on the lids of snuff-boxes, when the name of the wine is usually omitted. Among his engravings for plaques and boxes are magnificent representations of classical themes such as Danae and the Shower of Gold, Apollo and Daphne and Perseus and Andromeda. The mid-eighteenth century witnessed the flowering of neoclassicism which eventually became high fashion and ousted the rococo and romantic influences, replacing them by the turn of the century with the more disciplined Empire style. In 1755 the art historian, Johann Winkelmann, firmly declared that Greek art was 'the most perfect from the hands of man.'[10]

Other famous Ravenet engravings include Christ on the Cross, St James of Compostella, St Anthony of Padua, also portrait plaques of George III when Prince of Wales (after Richard Wilson), George II, and the Duke of Cumberland, the last among the rare pieces signed *Ravenet ft*. On close examination of that plaque at the British Museum the author found that the signature is faintly engraved in a somewhat naive manner, each letter being formed by unevenly spaced dots. This signature does not appear to match Ravenet's standard of engraving and it might have been added to the plate by another hand. Signatures on other pieces by Ravenet appear as *S. Rav. fecit*. A famous plaque is that of Henry Pelham, on which it is thought that Ravenet engraved only the face; it is possible that the clothing may have been engraved by Brooks. Ravenet's engravings of groups of Boucher-like cherubs show 'that generally gracious air of classic joys that only the France of the eighteenth century could paint and that Ravenet appears to have been so well able to adapt as decorations for enamels.'[11]

John Hall, who became Historical Engraver to George III, was apprenticed to Ravenet at the age of 15 in 1754, but would hardly have been able to produce much original work before the closing of the factory early in 1756. The chief artist employed at York House was yet another Irishman, James Gwin, or Gwim, who had been a coach painter in Kildare. He is thought to have been responsible for most of the designs which with any certainty can be attributed to Ravenet's engravings, particularly mythological and allegorical subjects. A rare enamel plaque, of Britannia encouraging linen manufacture in Ireland, was found with the following contemporary inscription on the back:

> 'Drawn by Gwin, engraved by Ravenet for ye Battersea Manuf're under Sir J. Theodore Janssen. Ye design a Compt. for Linen Manufacturers of Ireland during ye Lieutenancy of ye Duke of Dorset.'[12]

Gwin was also an engraver but none of his engravings have been identified as appearing on enamels.

A device which was featured on Battersea enamels was the Arms of the Anti-Gallican Society, formed in 1745 in order to discourage the importation and consumption of French

produce and manufacture. The design depicts St George spearing the lilies of France, surmounted by Britannia and flanked by the British lion and the Prussian eagle with the motto 'For Our Country' on a ribbon below. As the Society's Grand President, this was a cause close to Janssen's heart. It must have delighted him to be responsible for originating luxurious objects, for which he hoped there would be a ready market: they demonstrated the new technique developed in his factory and at the same time competed with the expensive toys being imported from France. In a memorandum to Newcastle on 10 January 1756, two days prior to his bankruptcy being declared, he claimed:

> 'He was the means of bringing in the bill for prohibiting cambrics during the late war with France, which has preserved a great quantity of our wealth from going into that kingdom.'[13]

Few names in the decorative arts have achieved lasting fame in so short a period as Battersea. In less than three years the enamels made there acquired a reputation for excellence, which has endured throughout the centuries.

Above left: A further example of a Battersea lid on a Birmingham base. In this instance there has been no attempt to match, either colourwise or stylistically, the lobed, flower-painted base to the lid. The interior of the lid bears a portrait, transfer-printed in puce, of Prince George, later George III, after Ravenet. The top of the lid is transfer-printed in puce with Britannia presenting a medal and surrounded by Arts and Sciences. (Halycon Days)
Above: A rare Battersea oval plaque of the arms of the Anti-Gallican Society, transfer-printed in gold. The arms depict St George spearing the *fleur-de-lis* of France, surmounted by Britannia and flanked by the British lion and Prussian eagle; on a ribbon below is the motto 'For our Country'. Height 8.2 cm (3¼ ins) (Halcyon Days)

THE IDENTIFICATION OF BATTERSEA ENAMELS

How is the genuine Battersea enamel to be identified? Bearing in mind that recognition of the fine quality milky-white enamel of the background is the first essential, the following points are the ones to look for:

ARTICLES *Plaques*—oval and rectangular, not more than 15 centimetres (6 inches) in any one measurement and usually around 10 centimetres (4 inches). *Boxes*—normally of rectangular form but some oval. Mounts always of fine quality, beautifully chased and gilded. *Bottle Tickets or Decanter Labels* —in the form of wavy escutcheons or cartouches.

Other articles were made, or at least decorated, at Battersea. There is a school of thought which maintains that enamels were only decorated there, that no actual enamelling was carried out but that ready-enamelled blanks were brought in from elsewhere, possibly from other London workshops, as were the mounts for boxes, the frames for plaques and other metal accessories. It is also probable that at least some of these were obtained from Birmingham or other Midland sources. It is significant that in the York House sale notice, stock and blank enamels are listed but there is no mention of copper shapes or of grinding mills or of other items of equipment essential to the manufacture of enamels. Crosses were among the items in the sale notice of Janssen's house contents and a very few Battersea crosses do exist, but they and articles other than the three principal groups listed are exceedingly rare.

SUBJECT MATTER Religious, mythological, classical, allegorical, emblematical, political, portraits of royalty and aristocracy. These do not cover the entire range of Battersea subjects, but although romantic and naturalistic themes were possibly used, they are generally more likely to figure on enamels from other sources.

STYLE OF DECORATION All Battersea enamels were transfer-printed on a white ground. The prints were of superlative quality, with fine, clearly defined lines. Examine under a magnifying glass a piece you consider a possibility. If the engraving is uneven, poorly defined or smudgy, it is almost certainly not a Battersea enamel. The colours known to have been used for printing were: soft mauve, reddish-brown, crimson, puce, purplish-brown, sepia, charcoal, gold and (rarely) silver. The majority were decorated in monochrome and occasionally added to with brushwork in the same colour as the print, but a very few were printed in two colours. Others, with the exception of those with metallic transfers, were carefully overpainted with delicate, translucent colours which allowed the fine, flowing unbroken lines of the design to show through and in no way obscured, but rather enhanced, the engravings. It has been suggested that a yellow ground was used at Battersea, but this was not so.

On lids of boxes and on plaques, the design invariably covered the entire area and was seldom enclosed within a decorative panel or border. Portraits were generally set simply on an undecorated background. The interior lids of boxes were often decorated, as were the interior and underside of their bases. A variety of diaper (diamond-shaped) patterns were used on side panels, usually within Louis XV-

Below left: Scenes of history and mythology, religious subjects, emblems and portraits appear on many Battersea enamels, but interior conversation pieces are very rare. This plaque, transfer-printed in red and overpainted, shows a gentleman and a lady of about 1750. Width 10 cm ($3\frac{7}{8}$ ins) (Victoria & Albert Museum)

style engraved frames. It must be borne in mind, however, that most of these features can be observed on enamels made elsewhere, probably in Birmingham; the subtle, deciding factor in favour of Battersea is one of superior quality.

It was obviously accepted practice that the different transfer-prints used to decorate a box bore no relation to each other. A typical box was decorated with Ravenet's engravings thus: on the lid, a print of The Trojan priest Laocoon with the horse of Troy; on the interior of the lid a portrait of Henry Pelham; around the sides, children as Arts, Science and Commerce, surrounded by panels composed of elaborate, very French rococo scrolls; and on the base, boys with the British lion, flag and shield.

Those at Battersea responsible for the selection of available engravings to place onto the seven or eight surfaces of a rectangular box apparently sought to satisfy all tastes.

Above: Venus begging arms from Vulcan for Aeneas, a rectangular Battersea plaque, after Simon-François Ravenet, transfer-printed in red and over-painted. Mythological subjects were very popular in mid-eighteenth century England and were used to decorate a large proportion of the enamels made at Battersea. Measuring 14 cm ($5\frac{1}{2}$ ins) in width, this is among the largest plaques thought to have been made there. Other versions of this subject exist some of them made in Birmingham. (Victoria & Albert Museum)

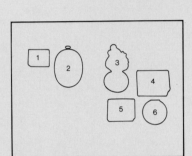

1 A snuff-box of 1760–65 painted
with a portrait of an unknown
lady from a mezzotint by Richard
Purcell (1736–66) after a painting
by Van der Mijn (1719–83). The
sides and base have sprays of
flowers on a raised gilt diamond
pattern. The portrait on this box
and that on the medallion of
George III on this page are the
work of a miniaturist of distinction
and the subjects featured indicate
that it was most probably one
resident in London. Length 6.1
cm (2⅜ ins) (Wolverhampton
Museum)
2 An oval medallion, *circa* 1761,
with a portrait of George III
after the painting by Thomas
Frye, the director of the Bow
porcelain factory (1710–62)
engraved by his pupil William
Pether (1731–95). The purple
scrolls which form the border are
often seen surrounding portraits,
including ones of inferior quality.
Height 11 cm (4⅜ ins)
(Wolverhampton Museum)
3 This Chelsea porcelain

bonbonnière of *circa* 1760 has
been photographed open, to
display its enamel base which
resembles item 4, a London snuff-
box. The same flowers as those
on the base of the *bonbonnière*
are continued on the inside of the
porcelain top. Diameter 5.4 cm
(2⅛ ins) (Halcyon Days)
4 This is a rare box as it is
marked on the base 'Anth.
Tregent Denmark Street, St
Giles'—a London firm whose
name is normally seen only on
monochrome transfer-printed
enamels; the lid and the
corrugated sides of this box are
painted with flower sprays in
natural colours. The base is
printed with a calendar from
July to December 1759. Length
9.2 cm (3⅝ ins) (Halcyon Days)
5 A London calendar box for
1758, the lid and base with the
two parts of the calendar and the
sides with feast days. The
interior of the lid is transfer-
printed in black with a trophy of
the Prussian eagle, above

the coats of arms of Austria
and France, with the motto '*Vive
Frederic le Grand*'. Length 6.5 cm
(2½ ins) (Lawrence Gould
Collection)
6 Experts disagree on whether
this box should be classified as
Birmingham or London. The
author favours the latter
attribution as there are other
boxes thought to have been made
in London which bear the same
style of Kakiemon flower painting
and similar fine quality mounts
with twisted rope thumb-pieces;
they all appear to have come
from the same workshop. The
Kakiemon pattern, which
originated in Hizen in Japan in
the seventeenth century, is seen
on many types of porcelain—
Meissen, Chantilly and Worcester
among others; it was also used at
Bow and Chelsea, two London
factories closely associated with
enamellers. Made *circa* 1755, its
diameter is 5.8 cm (2¼ ins)
(Wolverhampton
Museum)

London

There is much controversy about enamels attributable to London. An increasing number of those previously accredited to Midland sources are now thought to have been made in the metropolis by the many enamellers who were active there in the eighteenth century.

THE SOPHISTICATED crafts flourished in fashionable London in the mid-eighteenth century. The purveyors of cultivated luxury—the watchmakers, lapidaries, goldsmiths and jewellers—were constantly seeking innovations to impress their aristocratic, rich and famous clients. This atmosphere was ripe for the introduction of charming enamelled toys. At their best, the fine copper enamels produced in the capital bore favourable comparison with the gold-based objects of vertu they emulated.

From the early 1700s there had been extensive production of enamel dials for watches and clocks by London enamellers. At first these were simply painted with numerals but towards the mid-century they became increasingly elaborate and were decorated with landscapes, shipping scenes and all types of ornamental designs.

By the 1740s enamelling was widely practised in England but the fame of Battersea was soon to eclipse the achievements of craftsmen enamelling elsewhere in London—understandably perhaps as Battersea was unique, being a factory primarily devoted to the novel technique of transfer-printing. Although this was an original development in the decorative arts, 'it was a brave venture to offer to the London world plain engravings on white enamel. Like Gothic architecture, a line engraving only pleases when it is very good indeed.'[1]

At Battersea, transfer-printing was very good indeed and elsewhere it was ideal as an aid to mass-production. But in its monochrome state it did not satisfy all tastes and opportunities abounded for those who could create enamel objects which were brilliantly coloured. The names are known of at least 25 enamellers from a much larger number working in London between 1745 and 1770. Of one of these, George Michael Moser, 'Chaser and Painter in Enamel Colours, Craven Buildings, Drury Lane'[2] it was written: 'Moser was originally a chaser, but when that mode of decorating plate, cane-heads and watch-cases became unfashionable, he by the advice of his friend, Mr Thomas Grignion, the celebrated watchmaker, applied himself to enamelling . . .' Moser was the first Keeper of the Royal Academy from 1768 until his death in 1783. He was responsible for many fine enamels on gold and is particularly associated with those in the neoclassical style; it is doubtful, however, if he at any time painted copper-based enamels.

Many famous London miniaturists chose the medium of enamel, among them Christian Frederick Zincke, his pupil Jeremiah Myer, Samuel Cotes, Richard Crosse, Nathaniel Hone and his son Horace, Henry Bone, William Prewitt,

Gervase Spencer and Henry Spicer. Nevertheless, no copper-based enamel objects have been discovered which can be attributed to these artists. It is conceivable that, in their earlier periods, they might have been tempted to decorate enamel snuff-boxes and other trinkets, in the absence of more lucrative commissions. But if the mature work of well-known artists had appeared on copper enamel toys, their 'identity' would surely be revealed, just as their unsigned miniatures can be recognized.

Among the rare English enamels which are signed and dated is a small medallion in the Ionides Bequest at the Victoria and Albert Museum, signed on the back '*Jean Mussard à Londres*'. Jean Antoine Mussard, born in Geneva in 1707, came from a famous family of miniaturists and enamellers. In 1754, a firm by the name of Peter Mussard appears in the Apprenticeship Indentures at the Public Record Office in London as 'Jewellers of St. Martin-in-the-Fields'. Other names featured include Joseph Allen, who from 1742 to 1754 was recorded as a 'Snuffbox maker and Enameller of St Luke, Middlesex', and George Morris, described as a 'Goldsmith and Enameller' at Well-Close Square in 1750 and at Foster Lane in 1751–52.

On a trade card of about 1760 a man by the name of Morris, who was a goldsmith and toyman at the King's Arms, on the corner of Norris Street, in St James, Haymarket, advertised that he: 'Manufactured all sorts of Enamell'd work in Snuff Boxes, watches and chains, toothpick cases, trinkets . . .'[4] Another enameller, James Goddard, described himself thus: 'Enameller, Denmark Street, St Giles. The branch of Enamelling professed by this Artist is the painting in Enamel History, Figures and Flowers on watch cases, *Etwees* etc'[5] He was recorded as an enameller at different times from 1748 to 1763 and his output over a period of at least 15 years must have been considerable. A trade card of the mid-1760s stated that he enamelled 'Watch Cases, Snuff Boxes and Curious Work in Gold' as well as 'Dial Plates of all sizes for Clocks and Watches'. The dials would have been on copper, a significant point which shows that enamelling was carried out on copper and on gold in the same workshop.

In Denmark Street there was also a business owned by a Swiss man, Anthony Tregent. He is the best known of all London suppliers of copper-based enamels, for the simple reason that he was aware of the cachet attached to a marked piece: his enamels were signed 'Made by Anth. Tregent Denmark Street'. Born in Geneva in 1721, Tregent was one of three brothers who settled in London. One of them, James, was a watchmaker in Leicester Square. A clock in the Schreiber Collection in the Victoria and Albert Museum has an enamel dial with James Tregent's name on it. Anthony Tregent's daughter was buried in Battersea in 1752, indicating that he may have lived there. This has given rise to the theories that at one time he was involved in the manufactory at York House, and also that he supplied Janssen with blank white enamel box bases and lids for decorating. But it is by

Right: John Wilkes (1727–97) was a forceful and daring politician who championed the rights of the people. In his paper, *The North Briton*, he made so violent an attack on the government that he was committed to the Tower of London. He was later Member of Parliament for Middlesex and eventually became first Lord Mayor and then Chamberlain of the City of London. This box is on view in the British Museum, London where it is labelled 'of London or Midland manufacture'. Length 7.2 cm (2.0 ins)

no means certain that he was actually a manufacturer of enamels. The possibility exists that he was a shop owner only, and that enamels made elsewhere were especially marked with his name. This was common practice: many Continental and provincial English manufacturers of fashionable *objets* gained higher prices for their wares if they were marked 'London', with or without a maker's name, and consequently this subterfuge was rife.

Dated boxes and medallions provide a little of the evidence which is so rare in the study of English enamels. Anthony Tregent specialized in making table snuff-boxes, transfer-printed in monochrome, for specific occasions. Many of these are inscribed with almanacs for 1758, 1759 and 1760, giving the fixed and moveable feasts and the eclipses of the sun and moon. One, in the British Museum in London, is signed 'Anth. Tregent', inscribed 'A New Year's Gift' and dated 1759. Similar boxes, some of which were also marked with his name, were decorated with stanzas from popular songs, and others with Masonic insignia. Octavius Morgan M.P., the nineteenth-century antiquarian, owned one of the latter dated 5754 according to the Masonic calendar. By subtracting 4000, the Year of Masonic Light, 5754 would correspond to the date 1754. These are among the earliest dated English enamels. Similar articles were also produced in Birmingham and in Liverpool.

It is interesting to note that in the mid-eighteenth century there were several references to Chelsea in respect of enamel-

Right: This elegant snuff-box is painted with what appears to be a scene from a play with a lady and a gentleman in court dress of about 1750. On the sides are further scenes; one shows a lady with a gentleman in fancy dress, seated in a box at a theatre. The panels are enclosed within yellow rococo scrolls. On the base there is a painted rose spray. It is most likely that fine quality pieces decorated with sophisticated themes such as this were made in London. Length 7.5 cm (3 ins) (Victoria & Albert Museum)

ling. This London borough was mentioned by André Rouquet, a famous enameller who worked in the metropolis for nearly 30 years. He returned to the Continent about 1750 and settled in Paris. In 1755 he published a book, *L'Etat des Arts en Angleterre* in which he reported that on a visit to a manufactory near Chelsea he witnessed decoration *en camayeu par espèce d'impression* (in monochrome by a type of printing).

Chelsea was also named as a place where enamels were manufactured in an advertisement in the *Liverpool Advertiser* in 1757 which referred to transfer-printing 'as lately practised at Chelsea, Birmingham etc.' and it was stated that John Hall 'when a lad' worked for Ravenet at 'the manufactories then in high estimation at Chelsea, under the direction of Sir Stephen Jansen [sic]'.[6]

Although it is generally assumed that these references to Chelsea were mistaken, and that they really referred to Battersea, just across the river, it is probable that Janssen did not start from scratch at York House but that prior to 1753 he experimented with enamelling processes elsewhere, possibly in Chelsea. It is certain that enamellers were associated with Chelsea porcelain production as many delightful Chelsea porcelain toys incorporated enamelled components such as stoppers on porcelain scent bottles, bases on *bonbonnières* and lids on patch-boxes. Likewise enamel scent bottles exist with Chelsea porcelain birds as finials to their stoppers. Sometimes flower painting on the porcelain and on the enamel appears to be by the same hand. It would have been natural for painters who had worked at Chelsea to practise their skill on enamels in other London factories.

At that time the word enameller did not necessarily des-

cribe a maker of enamel boxes or toys. It could have referred to a miniaturist, or to one who worked exclusively on gold-based objects; although artists who decorated porcelain or pottery with enamel colours were usually referred to as 'painters', occasionally they too were called 'enamellers'.

William Hopkins Craft of Tottenham (1730–1811) was a famous enameller who at one time, when in partnership with another artist, David Rhodes, worked for Wedgwood in London. Craft's enamel plaques were generally on the grand scale and he specialized in portraiture, allegorical subjects and decorative compositions. It was said of him that he was 'very good in manipulation, but very weak in art'.[7] He was the brother of the Thomas Craft who was a painter at Bow porcelain factory. In the Irwin Untermeyer Collection in New York there is a pair of cassolettes attributed to Matthew Boulton of Birmingham with enamel domed covers painted with pastoral scenes; they are signed: W.H. Craft, 1787.

An advertisement in *Aris's Birmingham Gazette* on 5 November 1753 brings into perfect focus the climate which existed regarding those who decorated *objets d'art*:

'This is to give Notice to all Painters in the Blue and White Potting Way, and Enamellers on China-ware, that by applying at the Counting House at the China Works near Bow, they may meet with Employment and proper Encouragement, according to their Merit; likewise Painters brought up in the Snuff-Box Way, Japanning, Fan-painting, etc., may have Opportunities of Trial, wherein, if they succeed, they shall have due Encouragement . . .'[8]

Above: Four small, fine quality patch-boxes of a particularly shallow type which are attributed to London and are dated about 1755. The boxes are exquisitely painted, the oval ones with exotic birds and foliage in the *chinoiserie* style, the rectangular ones with flowers. There is a French inscription inside the base of each box. The yellow box shows radial corrugations which are often present on boxes considered to be of London origin. Average length 5.5 cm (2¼ ins) (Eric Benton Collection)

In a paper on The London Enamellers published by the English Ceramic Circle in 1972, Eric Benton expressed the view that several groups of enamels until then attributed to other sources, had been made in London workshops. Among the many different subjects reviewed was a portrait, frequently seen on English enamels, of the actress Mary Brooks. She was the wife of James Brooks, a line-engraver of Fleet Street and not, as was mistakenly assumed for many years, the wife of John Brooks, Janssen's partner at York House, Battersea. Finely painted facsimiles of this portrait appear on enamels attributable to London, including an *étui* and a snuff-box in the Schreiber Collection. Inferior versions of it are sometimes found on enamels of Midland manufacture.

In 1978 Mary Morris, who spent many years at Wolver-hampton Museum researching English enamels, drew the author's attention to a group of highly decorative, brilliantly coloured enamels, which she considered to be of London origin; their subject matter dates from about 1760. According to Mary Morris, these enamels were classified many years ago as Bilston when it became evident that they had been made after 1756, post-dating the closing of the Battersea factory. They are usually decorated with portraits of royalty or of famous people. The painting, which is very fine, is the work of a skilled miniaturist and, given the subjects selected, one most probably resident in London. It is unlikely that an artist of this calibre could have been working in Bilston and have remained unknown. Also, it seems improbable that there would have been a demand there for subjects as fashionable as the ones chosen.

A medallion of George III in Wolverhampton Museum and a companion medallion of Queen Charlotte are two of the most outstanding examples. Other portraits, apparently by the same hand, are seen occasionally on fine quality objects of a sophisticated nature. But there are many plaques, boxes, scent bottles and *étuis* which appear to be clumsy attempts at copying the palette and style of this artist, particularly the dark blue-grey background which is a feature of his work. These copies may well have been made in South Staffordshire at a later date.

Many styles of decoration were used on enamels which are considered of London origin. *Chinoiserie,* then high fashion, was expressed in oriental-style motifs, flowers and exotic birds. Risqué subjects were more likely to have found favour with a frivolous, mondaine society than in Midland areas where Puritan influences were strong. Some boxes with double lids, the inner one painted with a *scène grivoise,* bore exceedingly fine paintings of classical scenes on the exterior.

London was the home of the finest metal work of all kinds and also of watchmaking; the parts for the cases of watches are so similar to those required for enamel boxes. There is a particular diamond-chain patterned mount which is found on Chelsea porcelain toys and on enamel boxes. The accompanying inner rim is scalloped and the heavy gold plating has invariably endured in almost perfect condition throughout the centuries. This was the 'double-gilt' plating referred to in the York House sale notice, an expensive finish only used for top quality pieces. Those of lesser value are found today with dull bronze mounts, their inferior gilding having completely worn away.

Although London enamellers no doubt obtained some of their supplies of metal accessories from Midland manufacturers, most of their needs could easily have been met by local silversmiths, jewellers and other metal workers.

There is much controversy regarding the enamels attributable to London; for a piece to be considered of London origin, the essential attributes are superlative craftsmanship and sophistication of subject matter. London enamellers, in close touch with their discerning clients, were more likely to respond to personal whims and fancies than those in Midland areas who generally supplied their wares at arm's length.

Below: An unusual blue enamel scent bottle, of about 1765, painted in gold with sprays of flowers which exactly match those seen on other enamels thought to have been made in London. Height 6.4 cm (2½ ins) (Eric Benton Collection)

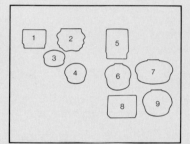

1 Two lovers in a pastoral setting—a recurrent theme on English enamels, naively interpreted in this small Birmingham snuff-box which is transfer-printed and overpainted. *Circa* 1765.

2 A cartouche-shaped Birmingham snuff-box; the lid, portraying children playing games, is in the typical pallette of soft colours found on Birmingham enamels made around 1750. The sides are delicately painted with flowers within auricular scrolls and there is a single rose painted on the base. The box has gilt metal mounts and a base rim; the latter is a sign of an early box, made before the art of covering right angles with enamel was generally mastered.

3 A small oval patch-box painted with summer flowers and sprays. This too has a base mount, but for decoration rather than as protection as this box dates from about 1770 by which time it was no longer necessary to cover edges.

4 A circular snuff-box of about 1760, the enamel lid painted with a quayside scene with raised gilt

scrolls and flowers on a white ground. The base of the box is of Sheffield plate and the underside is stamped with a flowered cartouche.

5 A rectangular Birmingham snuff-box of about 1760, transfer-printed in sepia. The engraving on the lid is *The Shepherd Lovers* after Louis P. Boitard. It shows a shepherd and a shepherdess embracing and, peering from behind a tree, an old woman wringing her hands at the sight. The sides are printed in sepia with a diaper design within scrollwork and on the base there is a print of *Comédie Italienne*, a subject engraved by Robert Hancock after a painting by Jean Antoine Watteau (1684–1721) and an engraving by C. N. Cochin (1715–90).

6 A snuff-box, probably made in Birmingham around 1755. *Chinoiserie* was then being used extensively for, among other things, the decoration of japanned ware, which was a Birmingham speciality. The painting on this box is in the style of Petrus Schenk, an early eighteenth-

century Dutch engraver whose work was used at Meissen. The sides and base bear painted flowers in a reduced pallette similar to those on the lid.

7 An oval snuff-box of about 1775 transfer-printed in charcoal. It is possible that this type of box, of which there were many, might have been produced in Liverpool as well as in Birmingham.

8 A Birmingham shallow rectangular snuff-box, fitted with French silver mounts of about 1744–50. The mounts are of a type found on enamel boxes made by Fromery of Berlin.

9 A shallow Birmingham snuff-box, the design painted in red outline and filled in with colours. All these boxes are illustrated actual size. (Halcyon Days)

Birmingham

Acknowledged as the world's most important centre for the manufacture of all things metallic, Birmingham also produced the widest variety of articles made in enamel in the eighteenth century, many of which were of great beauty and fine quality. It was from Birmingham that John Brooks made his first unsuccessful application to patent the invention of transfer-printing.

ALTHOUGH there is scant evidence to guide researchers, a clearer picture of the origins of eighteenth-century English enamels is slowly emerging. Whereas at one time they were all attributed to Battersea, as it was believed that the York House factory was the first and principal source, evidence now available shows clearly that Battersea enamels were comparatively few in number. Enamellers in London, Liverpool and Wednesbury were responsible for manufacturing considerable quantities of enamels, and the output from Bilston (the names are recorded of some 20 enamelling establishments there) was equalled only perhaps by that of Birmingham, dubbed by Edmund Burke as 'the great toyshop of Europe' and possibly the most prolific centre for the practice of the craft.

Birmingham was in the forefront of the Industrial Revolution. By the mid-eighteenth century it was already the most important centre in England for the production of all types of metal goods: steel, iron, silver, brass and copper, including copper blanks for enamelling, many of which were sent to other enamelling centres. It was particularly famous for the manufacture of buttons, immense quantities of which were made, and also snuff-boxes, patch-boxes and toys, many of them enamelled.

A visitor to Birmingham wrote in 1755: 'We saw the manufactory of Mr. Taylor, the most considerable maker of gilt-metal buttons, and enamelled snuff boxes.' This was John Taylor, a 'valuable acquaintance' of Dr Samuel Johnson, High Sheriff of Warwickshire in 1756, and one of the original founders, in 1765, of Lloyd's Bank.[1] Taylor was transfer-printing on enamels in 1766 when Lady Shelburne wrote of a visit to his factory:

> 'At Mr Taylor's we met again and he made an ennamel'd landscape on the top of a box before us which he afterwards gave me as a curiosity from my having seen it done. The method of doing it is this: a stamping instrument managed only by one woman first impressed the picture on paper, which paper is then laid even upon a piece of white enamel and rubbed hard with a knife, or instrument like it, till it is marked upon the box. Then there is spread over it with a brush some metallic colour reduced to a fine powder which adheres to the moist part and, by putting it afterwards into an oven for a few minutes, the whole is completed by fixing the colour.'[2]

Left: The marriage of King George III (1738–1820) to Charlotte Sophie, Princess of Mecklenburg-Strelitz (1744–1818) took place on 8 September 1761 and their coronation was held on 22 September of that year. It is thought that this box was made at the time in Birmingham or in London to celebrate the latter event. The lid is transfer-printed in pink with a portrait of the King after an engraving by William Woollett (1735–85). Inside the lid is a portrait of Queen Charlotte. A translation by Thomas Parnell from *Pervigilium Veneris* is inscribed on the base: 'Let him love now who never lov'd before. Let him who ever lov'd now love the more'. Length 8.3 cm (3¼ ins) (Reproduced by gracious permission of Her Majesty the Queen. Copyright reserved)

This was a form of bat-printing, which was one of the transfer-printing techniques used at the time.

In 1781 the Birmingham historian, W. Hutton, wrote of John Taylor in his *History of Birmingham* as: 'the uncommon genius to whom we owe the numerous race of enamels.' Referring to Taylor's painted snuff-boxes, Hutton reported that 'one servant earned £3.10.0d a week by painting them at a farthing each.' At this period, a working week comprised seven days of 14 hours each, which meant that the rate of painting was less than two minutes per box. A wage of £3.10.0d was a very high one in those days and would have enabled the painter to employ one or more assistants. Even so, to paint over 3000 boxes in one week is mass-production on a considerable scale and the artistic standard must indeed have been low. It is not certain that Hutton was referring to enamel snuff-boxes, as Taylor is known also to have manufactured japanned metal snuff-boxes, and these too required painting.

Not all of Taylor's products were of poor quality, however. Hutton also reports that a nobleman, of distinguished taste, made several purchases which included a toy of 80 guineas' value and, while paying for them, observed, with a smile, 'he plainly saw he could not reside in Birmingham for less than

£200 a day.'[3] On a visit to the city in 1760, Viscount Palmerston, after visiting several manufacturers, including Mr Taylor, wrote: 'The whole town has an air of opulence, business and populousness beyond almost any except London. . .'[4]

In 1755 Taylor employed about 500 people but a large proportion of them were engaged in the manufacture of buttons and other metal trinkets. As one of Birmingham's foremost manufacturers, his influence was considerable and he played a leading part in the affairs of the day. In 1759 he testified before a subcommittee of the House of Commons:

Right: The Gunning sisters were young and exceptionally beautiful and when they arrived from Ireland in the spring of 1750, they took fashionable London by storm. The eldest, Maria (far right), married the Earl of Coventry in 1752 and died of arsenic poisoning at the age of 27 in 1760, having used a cream containing arsenic as a cosmetic to whiten the skin. Elizabeth married first the Duke of Hamilton and after his death the Duke of Argyll. It is thought that both plaques were engraved in about 1751–52, and that they are after portraits painted by Francis Cotes (1725–70). Height 8.9 cm ($3\frac{1}{2}$ ins) (Wolverhampton Museum)

'There are two or three Drawing Schools established in Birmingham for the Instruction of youth in the Arts of Designing and Drawing and thirty or forty Frenchmen are constantly employed in Drawing and Designing.'[5]

Following Taylor's death in 1775 at the age of 64, James Watt, inventor of the steam engine, wrote to his partner, Matthew Boulton: 'John Taylor died the other day worth £200,000 without ever doing a generous action.'[6] A posthumous character assassination by one who obviously knew him well.

It was in Birmingham that the Irish engraver John Brooks, who in 1753 became a co-founder of the famous Battersea factory, claimed to have developed the technique of transferprinting. He made his first unsuccessful application for patent rights on 10 September 1751:

'humble petition of John Brooks of Birmingham in the county of Warwick, engraver, Sheweth that the petitioner has by great study application and expense found out a method of printing, impressing, and reversing upon enamel and china from engraved, etched and mezzotinto plates, and from cuttings on wood and mettle, impressions of History, Portraits, Landskips, Foliages, Coats of Arms, Cyphers, Letters, Decorations, and other Devices. That the said art and method is entirely new and of his own invention and for as much as it will be for the service of the public. . .'[7]

That Brooks, a year later, was actively engaged in commercial transfer-printing in Birmingham is shown by an advertisement in *Aris's Birmingham Gazette* of 27 November 1752:

'Such Gentlemen as are desirous of having WAITERS printed, may apply to John Brooks, Engraver in the New Church-Yard, Birmingham, who is willing not only to treat with them on reasonable Terms, but also engages to execute the work in the most elegant Manner, with Expedition, and further, to disabuse those Gentlemen, who, as he is assur'd, have been told to the contrary, that he never intended to encourage a Monopoly in that Branch of Trade.
N.B. He also recommends that his Work may not be spoil'd, by committing it into the Hands of unskilful Daubers.'[8]

'Waiter' was the name used for a salver or a small tray. Those referred to would have been made of japanned metal.

It is currently thought that it was Brooks who sparked off the revolution in ceramics, including enamels, that allowed a wide public to be able to afford cheaper but nonetheless attractive artefacts. This had become possible following the innovation of the new process which enabled a single design to be duplicated many times. After he had moved to Battersea, Brooks made two further unsuccessful petitions, in January 1754 and in April 1755. By this last date he was no longer a partner at York House but he was apparently still connected with the factory.

An advertisement on 16 September 1751, in *Aris's Birmingham Gazette* underlines the fact that enamelling was already a

Above: In the early days of the enamel trade in Birmingham, many boxes were made with enamelled lids and bases of other substances.
Above left: a basket-shaped snuff-box, the gilt metal base chased to resemble wicker-work. The painting on the lid is taken from an engraving after Philips Wouwerman. Diameter 6.2 cm (2⅜ ins)
Above right: A rare snuff-box with a base of aventurine glass *en cage* within a chased metal frame. Marbleized glass and flower-painted enamel fused together decorate the tortoiseshell-lined lid. Length 6.2 cm (2⅜ ins) (Victoria & Albert Museum)

widespread trade in the Midlands by the time that transfer-printing was introduced.

'Abraham Seeman, Enamelling Painter, at Mrs Weston's in Freeman St. Birmingham, makes and sells all sorts of enamelling colours, especially the Rose Colours, likewise all sorts for China Painters. N.B. Most of the eminent Painters of Birmingham, Wednesbury and Bilston have made use of the above colours to their satisfaction.'[9]

Birmingham Trade Directories from the 1750s onwards list the names of more than a dozen men who were 'enamel manufacturers' and 'Toy Makers and Enamel Button Manufacturers'. In 1757, Bishop Pococke writing from Wolverhampton remarked that 'the people of Birmingham enamel in great perfection and cheap.'[10]

At this time, in Birmingham and the nearby Black Country —an area which has always nurtured the skilled and dextrous—there were innumerable resourceful, creative men who were quick to take advantage of the new technology which was evolving. Machinery was devised for small-scale production of artefacts which previously could only have been made individually by hand. It is the use of metal as an equal partner to enamel, rather than as a subsidiary appendage, that is most noteworthy, and particularly so in the case of boxes.

In the early years of the industry, before thin copper forms were easily available, a delightful variety of boxes of enamel combined with metal was made in many ingenious styles, sometimes with a third substance being incorporated, such as tortoiseshell, mother-of-pearl, hardstone, glass or pressed horn. Metals including brass, pinchbeck, copper, Sheffield plate, iron and tin, were pressed, stamped, turned, cast, chased, engraved, rose-engine turned, gilded, silvered or japanned and finally assembled with enamel lids or plaques. Before enamelling became fashionable boxes similar to these had been made with agate, lapis lazuli or other hardstone panels set into their lids.

Among the most charming were small basket-shaped boxes, the bases chased to appear as wicker, with small pannier handles of twisted wire attached at each side of the mount. Sometimes the enamel lid would be decorated with appropriate flowers, at other times with elaborate subjects such as Venetian or Neopolitan scenes. Boxes of this type can usually be dated prior to 1765. Basket-shaped boxes were later made completely in enamel, still employing the pannier mounts.

From the 1750s the japanning industry flourished in Birmingham, London, Wolverhampton, Usk and Pontypool. Fine japanned caskets and toilet boxes were made with Birmingham enamel plaques set into the lids. These plaques were usually magnificent pieces, painted with extensive views of landscapes with classical ruins and the much favoured Mediterranean port scenes, some of which were based on Visentini's engravings after Canaletto. The complete articles were almost certainly entirely of Birmingham manufacture, but such was the fame of Pontypool japanned metal that it was often assumed that the caskets were made there. It has even been suggested that there was an enamelling factory at Pontypool, in Monmouthshire, but this was not the case.

Left: A Birmingham plaque painted with a scene of an Italian *Veduta* after the style of Piranesi, with Roman ruins, statues and columns in the foreground leading onto a harbour scene with mountains in the distance. The plaque is set into a casket with gilt strap and arabesque work on the black japanned ground, and dates from about 1755. Large caskets such as this were often fitted with a set of four toilet boxes, constructed in a similar style. The enamel plaques on the smaller boxes were each painted in a similar manner, but with different scenes. Length 25 cm (10 ins) (Halcyon Days)

Among the enamels once attributed to Battersea which are now, as a result of recent research, credited to Birmingham is the famous plaque made for the Free British Fishery Society, which was founded in October 1750. Although Janssen, who founded the Battersea factory in 1753, was the Society's Vice President, it is believed that the poor quality and the powdery appearance of the outlines of the print—of a Watteau-like stylized country scene, designed by Louis P. Boitard—and the heavy overpainting, indicate both a pre-Battersea date and characteristics which are associated with Birmingham. It is considered that the printing of the design was inferior due to the lack of mastery of transfer-printing materials and techniques, rather than to an indifferently engraved plate. Bernard Watney has suggested that the plaque was made in Birmingham prior to 1753 'to catch Janssen's eye, as it were, and to encourage him to establish a London factory.'[11]

A print on paper of the same design, in reverse, appears in a small drawing book which was discovered in the British Museum in London. The book contains six designs, two of which are signed 'Boitard delin. Hancocks sculp' and another, 'R. Hancock Sculp.' The date of publication was 1754, but it is thought that the designs were used prior to this as they

Right: A rare Birmingham oval tobacco box, transfer-printed and overpainted *en camaieu* in brick red. The designs are by Robert Hancock and Louis P. Boitard and include *Minuet by the Sea*, *The Singing Lesson*, and *The Fishing Party*. These are among the group of designs which has been called by Bernard Watney 'The Swan Group', as they and others in the same category are sometimes found with an overpainted pair of swans in the foreground. *Circa* 1751–56. Height 9.5 cm (3¾ ins) (Lawrence Gould Collection)

are printed in reverse; the picture would have appeared the right way round when transferred to enamel.

The association of enamels with Robert Hancock, a man who became a famous partner in the firm of Worcester Porcelain, has always been somewhat hazy. In 1865, it was observed that a watch back in the Works Museum at the Worcester porcelain factory was decorated with a transfer-print of *The Tea Party* which was signed 'R.H.f.' As at this time, all English enamels were designated 'Battersea', it was naturally assumed that Hancock had worked there. When, in 1924, Bernard Rackham revised the catalogue of the Schreiber Collection at the Victoria and Albert Museum, he questioned this assumption. It is now thought that even though Hancock might have spent some time in London, his engravings were not used at Battersea and that before moving to Worcester in about 1756 he was principally engaged in engraving for the decoration of enamels in Birmingham and other Midland centres. Hancock and Boitard, who were both artists as well as engravers, were responsible singly and together for a great number of the transfers on Birmingham enamels. Some of their designs, which were overpainted in brilliant colours, had a pair of swans painted in the foreground. Similar designs to these were used to decorate plaques and snuff-boxes but without the painted swans. This associated group of enamels, which date from *circa* 1751 to *circa* 1756, has been named by Bernard Watney 'The Swan Group'.[12] It includes subjects such as *Les Fêtes Venitiennes*, The

Fortune Teller, The Singing Lesson, The Round Game, Peeping Tom, The Fishing Party and The Shepherd Lovers. The Boitard-Hancock subjects were mostly inspired by the eighteenth-century French romantic artists Boucher, Lancret, Claude Lorraine, Watteau, Nattier and Fragonard. In those days engravers and decorators frequently adapted designs taken from popular prints and paintings, which were freely plagiarized without acknowledgement to the originators. Artists were completely unprotected from having their work copied until 1842 when an act was passed which afforded them some protection.

In Birmingham, between 1751 and the end of the eighteenth century, there were at least six firms of enamellers, in addition to at least four individual enamellers and four manufacturers of enamel buttons. Among the men involved in these enterprises were Isaac Whitehouse, William Godfrey, Richard Askew (who had painted porcelain at Chelsea and Derby), George Spilsbury, John Hazeldine, John Vale, Abraham Seeman or Seaman (an enamel miniaturist of note) and Charles Richards, who was in business with his son and who supplied Matthew Boulton with enamels at some date before 1782. In 1769, Josiah Wedgwood described Boulton as the 'first manufacturer in England'.[13] At the Soho Manufactory, just outside Birmingham, which he started with John Fothergill in 1762, he at one time employed nearly a thousand people. His magnificent ormolu clocks, vases, candelabra and other decorative pieces were made to designs furnished by the Adam brothers and quite a few of the articles he produced incorporated enamel. The very size of the enterprise perhaps led to the assumption that enamels were made at Soho, but no conclusive evidence exists to confirm this, although in correspondence Boulton inferred that it was the case. An inventory taken at Soho in 1782 shows that Matthew Boulton had no enamelling shop at that time, although he had a small stock of enamels in his warehouse which had been made elsewhere and which included some articles from Wednesbury. (The Soho factory should not be confused with Soho, London).

In the collection of the late Queen Mary, there was a double enamel snuff-box with a silver-gilt mount struck with Boulton's hallmark for 1783 and also an enamel *étui* containing a gilt metal spoon stamped with the maker's initials 'B & F.' These items are rare and it would appear that as enamelling was being carried out in such profusion in Birmingham, Boulton found it expedient to sub-contract this work. Small enamel patch-boxes inscribed 'A trifle from

Below: A candlestick decorated in a style known as the 'Honeysuckle Group' in which the flower is the dominant motif of an all-over raised pattern on a contrasting background. It is considered to be of Birmingham or London origin. Height 27.5 cm (11 ins) (Halcyon Days)

Soho' are often found but these are typical of late eighteenth-century Bilston manufacture; they were probably given as gifts to visitors to the Soho factory.

The craft continued in Birmingham into the 1840s, by which time it had all but ceased everywhere else. In 1839, Robson's Directory listed three Birmingham enamellers: Charles Gwynne, J. Abrahall and John Brown and Co.

Birmingham possibly produced the widest variety of articles made in enamel in the eighteenth century. Many of them were more usually made in silver or in plate, and they were not attempted by enamellers elsewhere. Output increased considerably from the 1780s, when new and improved kilns were introduced, with the advantage that larger items could be fired in one piece.

Extraordinary mustard pots were made, the lids in sculptured form as knights in armour, the bases decorated with painted military trophies. No doubt *bonbonnières* in animal, vegetable and human forms were made in Birmingham as well as in Bilston, the centre with which these are more readily associated. Although Birmingham snuff-boxes and patch-boxes appeared in many shapes and sizes, there was a predominance of small circular boxes of simple form, with gently waisted sides. The standard of decoration ranged from fine interpretations of the works of great artists to the

Above: Two views of a magnificent serpentine-shaped cutlery box which echoes in style those made in wood about the same time, 1770. This was probably of Birmingham manufacture; the flower sprays on the 12 knives and forks as well as the floral festoons and sprays on the case are taken from illustrations in *The Ladies Amusement*. The painted scenes of distant views by the sea are enclosed within gilt scrolled frames and the engraved and chased gold-plated mounts are of fine quality. Height 25 cm (9⅞ ins) (Private Collection)

crudest daubing, obviously executed by the like of Mr Taylor's 'farthing-a-box' workers.

The majority of enamels attributed to Birmingham were decorated on a white background which extended over the entire surface area. For rococo and baroque frames, borders and cartouches, a limited number of colours were used, either in monochrome or with two or more colours combined, such as puce, purple, a reddy pink, rust, yellow or brown. There are a few decorative features which are recognizable instantly as Birmingham in origin; among these are a delicately painted moss rose, butterfly and bee design, trailing flowers within auricular scrolls, and a variety of insects painted on the undersides of small boxes, which might possibly be the signature of particular artists.

A rare type of decoration, thought to have been produced in Birmingham, consists of all-over silver floral motifs on a turquoise or green background. This was achieved by the application of platinum and was used principally on candlesticks of neoclassic form, similar to ones produced in metal by Matthew Boulton in around 1790. It has not, however, been proved that these were made in England; it is considered possible that they could have been manufactured in Germany or even in Russia.

Birmingham manufacturers have always been adept at catering for export markets and the enamellers were no exception. Boxes were made which featured the Empress of Russia (an enemy of England at that time), with appropriate

Cyrillic inscriptions, and others commemorated the battles of Frederick the Great. Plaques, medallions and boxes decorated with religious subjects, such as the Arms of Pope Clement XIII (1758–69), the Saints, and the series from the Passion, were obviously intended for export to Ireland or the Continent, as there would have been little demand for them in an actively Protestant country.

Throughout the years, many fine English enamels have been discovered in Russia as well as in most Continental countries. Matthew Boulton was very export-minded; he sent samples of his wares to St Petersburg from 1772 onwards and achieved good sales there. Metal 'toys' constituted a sizeable part of his production and being an exceptionally astute, highly successful businessman, he certainly would not have overlooked the potential sales of colourful enamelled novelties which could be culled from new markets. In 1776 he is reputed to have stated, however, that some countries were not worth the trouble and that there was no demand for elegant things in America or even in some parts of Germany.

Enamel boxes are sometimes found with lids of a quality and style different from their bases; these were put together by factors who bought in parts made by others and assembled them, ready for sale. The plater who placed the following advertisement in *Aris's Birmingham Gazette* on 22 March 1756 was probably following this practice:

> 'To be Sold extremely Cheap, *An Assortment of Enamel Goods*, with some utensils for the Enamel Business: The Goods chiefly consist of square and round Tops and Bottoms for Boxes of different Sizes, some painted and some plain; there are a few with Mounts. The Whole are in the Possession of Daniel Winwood, Plater, in Charles Street, Birmingham, who will shew the same, with an Inventory, or send Specimens to any one who shall be desirous of buying.'[14]

In describing recognizable features of Birmingham enamels, it must be borne in mind that this great centre of the metal manufacturing industries was a focal meeting point for enamellers and there can be no doubt that there was a considerable exchange of information on techniques and styles. This interchange of ideas is responsible for the similarities which exist between enamels from different areas. It is also the reason why experts often find it impossible to state with complete confidence exactly where an article was made.

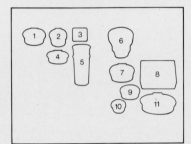

1 This romantic little box inscribed *'Gage d'amitié sincère'*, with a heart-shaped motif has the appearance of one made in the 1770s. But the mount is machine-made and the form of the lid and base less elegant than the souvenir boxes made at that time, indicating that it was probably produced about 1830.

2 A circular Bilston pill box of about 1790 with a lobed base; the lid is painted in pink *en camaieu* with a pastoral scene.

3, 4 'A Lover's Gift' and 'A Present from Bilston' are typical examples of the ubiquitous motto patch-boxes which were made in large quantities in Bilston during the last quarter of the eighteenth century.

5 A pencil, ivory slips, a penknife, a snuff spoon, a bodkin and scissors are fitted into this *étui* of tapering form. Made around 1770, it is decorated with painted lakeside and country scenes against a typically Bilston pink background.

6 *Bonbonnières* in the form of human heads were made in a wide variety of designs and styles; smiling blackamoors featured in many eighteenth-century designs. Made around 1770, this one is shown wearing a colourful turban. On the lid is an exterior scene enclosed within a rococo border, transfer-printed in pink and overpainted, showing a negro boy holding a French hunting horn, with a dog beside him.

7 A late eighteenth-century South Staffordshire snuff-box, the lid painted with a seated lady playing with a bird, within a gilt chevron border.

8 *Harlequin and Pierrot* after an engraving by Charles-Nicholas Vivares (1709–80) is the main subject used to decorate this rectangular snuff-box. The engraving is based on a fragment of a painting by Jean Antoine Watteau (1684–1721) depicting a scene from the Commedia dell'Arte. On the sides and base are flower-painted vignettes; the background of the box is deep blue with raised white rococo scrolled borders and embellishments.

9 A small oval patch-box with a painted spray of summer flowers on the lid and a lobed base enamelled in pink. The lid is mirror-lined and the box was made in the 1790s.

10 A small circular pill box of a type made in the early 1800s. The lid is transfer-printed and crudely coloured with figures symbolizing Charity.

11 An oval snuff-box of superior quality with an unusual maroon-coloured background. The lid is well painted with a pastoral scene which appears to be the work of a particular artist who always included a group of sheep with predominating shadows in the foreground of his pictures; there are sprays of flowers within reserves on the waisted base. All the boxes on these two pages are shown actual size. (Halcyon Days)

South Staffordshire

Second only to Battersea, the fame of
Bilston in South Staffordshire has endured
in the history of English enamels.
Although Bilston is particularly associated
with little boxes bearing inscriptions, many
larger enamels of distinction were
produced there and in nearby
Wednesbury.

Right: A writing box which illustrates to perfection the relaxed elegance of South Staffordshire enamels at their best. It is fitted with compartments and contains two glass inkpots. The lid is painted with a pastoral scene showing a hay cart in the foreground. On the side panels there are vignettes painted with scenes from *The Ladies Amusement. Circa* 1765. Length 18.5 cm (7½ ins) (By gracious permission of Her Majesty Queen Elizabeth, the Queen Mother)

ILSTON and Wednesbury were the two great centres for enamelling in South Staffordshire that have gained particular renown. Before the art of painted enamels came to Britain, Bilston was noted for the making of shoe buckles, metal boxes, trinkets and hinges. Japanners on metal were working there in the late 1690s and were specialists in making and decorating snuff-boxes with pull-off lids. The French craftsmen who fled to England from religious persecution in France and who chose to settle in Bilston undoubtedly did so because the town's metal-working industries were well suited to receive the associated field of manufacturing— enamelling on metal.

A number of French enamellers had settled there by 1745 and possibly earlier. By this date records show that enamels were being made in Bilston by a British craftsman named Dovey Hawkesford who died in 1749. A famous local family of enamellers, established prior to 1750, were the Bickleys, who were related to Hawkesford. On the death of both Benjamin Bickley and his son, John, in 1776, a sale was held of 'the tools and utensils necessary for carrying on the Enamel Business. . .'[1] Two years later, on the winding up of the estate, the equipment to be sold included a pair of millstones and two grinding mills which, running a normal 14-hour day, would have ground sufficient enamel powder to keep a considerable work force busy. A treasure trove of Bickley enamels was discovered in the attic of John Bickley's house, Ettinshall Lodge, nearly a century after he died. These were apparently sold and dispersed, so that the proof of their origin is now lost.

Trade Directories from 1760 onwards list 18 premises in Bilston where enamelling work was done. Another notable family in this profession were the Becketts. Isaac Beckett had a factory in Duck Lane, which was the old name for the present Queen Street. An Edward Beckett (1784–1831) had a factory in Bridge Street where the enamel factory of James Brett was also located. Other workshops in the area were owned by Thomas Perry, S. Hanson, J. H. Foster, John Vardon, John Simmons, Isaac Smith, Thomas Knowles and John Buckley. Edward Beckett struggled to keep the trade going despite the depression that followed the Napoleonic wars, and in 1827 he was the only remaining Bilston enameller to be recorded. When he died, his widow Susannah succeeded for a time in keeping the craft alive, but the last reference to her is in the 1835 Trade Directory, where she was listed as an enamel box maker. In Halcyon Days' collection there is a small oval box lid inscribed 'Er Becketts lid'. This might have indicated a particular style of decoration or perhaps it was a private joke in the factory.

Although clear evidence of the place of origin of a given enamel or of the craftsman responsible for it can be established only in the case of a few very rare pieces, occasionally it is possible to recognize the hand of a particular artist, such as one who painted sheep with predominating shadows.

One small patch-box in the collection at Wolverhampton Museum can be attributed to the Beckett family. It shows a transfer-print of Sam Proud's house and the message 'A trifle from Bilston'. Sam Proud was keeper of the local lunatic asylum and was related to the Beckett family. The box can be dated at approximately 1770 due to the particular type of steel mirror inside the lid. Of the untold thousands of small so-called Bilston boxes made through the years, this and the one inscribed 'Er Becketts lid' are the only examples known to the author that can be identified with a specific Bilston factory. It should be noted that, whereas glass mirrors

Left: Two extremely rare transfer-printed articles of Bilston enamel which can be traced to the factory of Edward Beckett, one of the town's leading enamellers. The small oval lid has a scene of a stag hunt. The box on the right, 'A Trifle from Bilston', has the words 'Sam Proud's House' printed on the ground in front of the house. Sam Proud was related to the Becketts and so it is naturally assumed that this box was made in their factory. *Circa* 1770. Length 4.3 cm (1⅝ ins) (Halcyon Days; Wolverhampton Museum)

Right: These two boxes demonstrate how a style of painting can be debased when copied. The larger box, made around 1770, is a fine example of the work of a Bilston artist who excelled at pastoral scenes in which there was usually a group of sheep with shadows. On the small navette-shaped oval patch-box of about 1790–1800 there is a group of sheep in the foreground, barely recognizable as such due to the inferiority of the painting. The length of the larger box is 7.7 cm (3 ins) (Wolverhampton Museum; Halcyon Days)

were introduced from about 1785 onwards, the use of steel mirrors continued until the 1790s.

Small Bilston boxes with inscriptions are perhaps the single most instantly recognizable group of typically English enamels. Although generally referred to as patch-boxes, if there was a mirror inside the lid, or as snuff-boxes if there was not, it is probable that many of these were principally intended as charming decorative objects to be displayed in cabinets or on small tables rather than to be used. They are collected more than any others, probably because there are so many different types from which to choose for specialized collecting. Romantic messages abound; 'Who opens this Must have a kiss', 'If you love me don't deceive me', 'I love but you' and lengthier pronouncements such as:

> 'With me you shall have no more pain,
> For I your sorrows will sustain,
> And it will be my daily care
> Your sorrows and your pains to share'.

Tokens of esteem and regard, trifles which show affection and friendship, and other similar sentiments were expressed, sometimes in misspelt French. It was considered chic to use French, all things Continental being fashionable in those days. Generally oval in shape but sometimes circular or rectangular, and measuring less than five centimetres (two inches) across, many of these boxes were decorated with pictures which related to the inscriptions—doves and hearts being particular favourites. The earlier ones dating from about 1770 were the most elegant, with meticulously transfer-printed and painted motifs; around 1790 Adam-style swags and borders were much in evidence; from 1800 onwards, the calligraphy and quality of decoration deteriorated rapidly.

Left: Royal occasions were
not always marked by
boxes of fine quality. The
Bilston box on the far left
is inscribed with 'Princess
Charlotte died Nov 6th
1817'. Britannia is seated
on the left, and on the right
an angel holds a tablet
inscribed: 'SHE'S gone to
the Palace above'. The oval
box was issued during
George III's illness and
bears the inscription:
Georgius III Rex. Blest by
the Eye of Providence the
King Enjoys a
Convalescence THANK
GOD! *Circa* 1810. Height
4.6 cm (1⅞ ins) (Halcyon
Days)

Among the many popular subjects used were views, often
of spas, with inscriptions such as: 'A present from Malvern',
or maybe Buxton or Harrogate. Sometimes an inscription
only was used. New and wonderful constructions such as The
Iron Bridge or The Pavilion, Brighton, were also in vogue;
shopkeepers had their names and a picture of the shop placed
on the lids of boxes as suitable gifts for esteemed clients.
Themes political, theatrical, humorous and bawdy were used
as well as those made in memoriam, and the little box was a
perfect medium to commemorate historical events, battles
won and royal happenings. The vicissitudes of George III's
illness resulted in a flood of boxes referring to 'Our Monarch's
Health'. Base shapes of motto boxes were either straight,
gently concave or *bombé* and corrugated and were enamelled
either in solid colours, usually leaving the underside white, or
decorated in multi-coloured patterns or stripes on a white
background.

Tantalizing joke boxes were made, such as one apparently
decorated with an unevenly shaped vase, its outline com-
prising the facing silhouettes of George IV and Queen
Caroline. Puzzle snuff-boxes had hidden, intricate closures
to their mounts which required a certain combination of
manoeuvres to open them. Refinements in snuff-taking led
to the development of perfumed snuff, for which double
boxes were made with two compartments, one for the scented
snuff and the other for the plain.

Apart from small boxes, the word Bilston conjures up
marvellous colours and lavish decoration on a wide range of
fascinating objects, from engaging small trinkets to large
pieces of considerable style and distinction. Bilston enamels
were the epitome of eighteenth-century charm. It has been
suggested that the different times at which colours were

introduced on enamels synchronized with those used on Chelsea porcelain, which were imitative of Sèvres. There is, nevertheless, considerable and conclusive evidence of a wide palette of colours having been used prior to the relevant dates. At Sèvres, dark blue *(bleu du roi)* was introduced in 1749, a light turquoise *(bleu celeste)* in 1752, yellow *(jaune jonquille)* in 1753, pea-green in 1756 and, in 1757, the famous *rose Pompadour*, miscalled rose du Barry in England. However, rose colours were referred to in Abraham Seeman's 1751 advertisement in *Aris's Birmingham Gazette* as being then available and being in demand by 'enamellers in Bilston, Birmingham and Wednesbury'. Pinks and reds are colours made from gold oxides, and recent experience at Bilston, since the revival of the craft, has shown how difficult they are to achieve. They cannot be mixed or toned down with the addition of white, as most other colours can, since they turn grey if white is added. In 1765 the Society of Arts offered prizes for new formulae for white and red enamels to replace those being imported from Venice, which was then the principal source of supply of enamel powders. It was in 1780 that a cheaper version of *rose Pompadour* was developed, a chrome-tin pink, known by Continental enamellers who imported it as English pink. Eventually almost every imaginable colour was used: lavender, plum, orange, apricot and wonderful shades of blues, greens and yellows. The panache with which these colours were employed can be observed in any comprehensive collection of English enamels.

Subjects which decorated South Staffordshire eighteenth-century enamels were largely taken from prints of famous paintings and books of engravings of which the most popular was *The Ladies Amusement; Or Whole Art of Japanning Made Easy* published about the period 1758–62 by Robert Sayer in Fleet Street, London. Its 200 plates showed over sixteen hundred different designs. These were by many artists, including Jean Pillement, whose flowers and romantic set-pieces were perfect designs for enamels; John June, an engraver who had executed some subjects after Hogarth; C. H. Hemerich, a German engraver who contributed *A Collection of Curious Insects*; Peter Paul Benazech, a pupil of Vivares; Charles Fenn, an artist who taught drawing in Birmingham in 1747 and who lived in a house next door to John Taylor's enamel and button-making establishment, and Robert Hancock. A famous engraving of exotic birds with an overturned basket of fruit, a favourite design with enamellers, was among the signed Hancock drawings which appeared. *The Ladies Amusement* was a wonderful source of elegant vignettes and motifs

Below: Bodkin cases were made in many amusing forms; this one is painted as a man wearing a pink cap and a purple and turquoise shawl. On the base, two hearts are aflame within a scrolled cartouche through the top of which runs a ribbon bearing the inscription '*Brulant du même feu*'. Made in about 1765. Height 12.9 cm (5 ins) (Halcyon Days)

and included innumerable versions of classical ruins, pastoral vistas, people engaged in country pursuits, *chinoiserie*, ornamental motifs, flowers, fruit, butterflies, birds and animals. Other useful publications providing artistic references were *Drawing Books* published by John Bowles during the period 1756–58, *The Draughtsman's Assistant*, published by Carrington Bowles in 1772, and *The Artist's Vade Mecum* published by Robert Sayer and J. Bennett in 1776.

The principal pictures chosen for the decoration of a piece, either hand-painted, transfer-printed, or printed and overpainted, would be set into reserves enclosed within elaborate panels of raised enamel scrolling, either white or gilded. Matching embellishments on the surrounding coloured backgrounds took various forms: simple diaper patterns, dot-and-dash designs or star-shaped motifs. Sometimes painted flower sprays would be interspersed. The finished box, inkwell, *étui*, tea caddy or candlestick was an imaginative and sumptuous *objet d'art*, excelling in many instances the Sèvres porcelain style of decoration which was the original inspiration.

Among the most light-hearted enamels attributed to Bilston, which are much sought after today, are the embossed scent bottles and *bonbonnières*, made in the form of animals, birds, human heads and figures, fruits, flowers, vegetables, shoes, musical instruments and groups of artist's impedimenta. Spaniels and cats on cushions were particularly fashionable and were among the more successful exports. The lids, which were the undersides of these *bonbonnières*, were often painted with scenes that reflected the three-dimensional subject. Other *bonbonnières* were joined to a scent bottle, the two forming a prettily shaped single piece.

Above: Robert Hancock's signature appears on the page in *The Ladies Amusement* which features this print of birds with an overturned basket of fruit. The small South Staffordshire box bears an engraving of the same subject, transfer-printed in red and overpainted in brilliant colours. The picture is reserved on a dark blue background with raised white decoration. There are enamels decorated with this same design in the Schreiber Collection and in the Irwin Untermeyer Collection in New York. Length 6 cm ($2\frac{1}{4}$ ins) (Halcyon Days)

Above: Embossed trophy *bonbonnières* were among the amusing toys made in the 1770s. These depict, with mottoes often in misspelt French, from left to right: hunting motifs, inscribed *A la chasse amoureuse*; musical instruments and the song *Ariette*, inscribed *Toujours le Zephyr Plus gay*; and a group of artist's impedimenta inscribed *Piendra vos bautes*. All measure approximately 5.5 cm (2¼ ins) across. (Lawrence Gould Collection; Halcyon Days)

When Bernard Rackham catalogued the Schreiber Collection at the Victoria and Albert Museum in 1924 he classified as Battersea 'Small scent bottles and snuff-boxes made in the shape of birds, animals or heads of the same, fruit or other natural objects in emulation of the similar articles being made at the same time in porcelain at Chelsea.' Rackham then added a footnote which explained that it had been brought to his attention that a copy of the *Gentleman's Magazine* of 1760 contained a notice announcing the first edition of *The Ladies Amusement*. This had forced him to reconsider the division of enamels between Battersea and Staffordshire and he was compelled to ascribe a larger number of enamels to the latter area. Subsequently, it became accepted generally that the source of their manufacture was Bilston as this appeared to be the most likely alternative to Battersea.

In 1966, in a paper published by the English Ceramic Circle, R. J. Charleston, Keeper of Ceramics at the Victoria and Albert Museum, and Bernard Watney, a leading authority on English enamels, proved that Birmingham was a centre equal to any other for the manufacture of enamels. It therefore became a possibility that embossed articles in natural forms could have been made there. In 1972 Eric Benton focussed attention on London where, in addition to the impetus given to designers by a fashionable Georgian public, there was an unequalled pool of talent: fine metal workers to create the components, enamellers to enamel them and artists of high calibre to decorate them.

All types of enamels vary enormously in quality, as obviously they were produced to be sold in various price brackets, but the best of the toys are superbly made. Future research might well reveal that many of these *bibelots* were made in London and that not all were made in the Midlands.

W EDNESBURY, the other important centre of enamelling in South Staffordshire and only six kilometres (three and a half miles) from Bilston, was little more than a village in the mid-eighteenth century. Metal working was a local industry and glazed pottery had been made there since the seventeenth century. By 1800 it was a small country town with a population of around 4000. Today, an almost continuous industrial belt, which is generally known as the Black Country, stretches from Wolverhampton to Birmingham and encompasses Bilston, Darlaston, Wednesbury and West Bromwich.

Enamelling, in common with most crafts, can be successfully pursued by one person or can be carried out by an integrated work force of ever increasing size. It follows that being in such close proximity to Bilston, some enamellers who worked there but lived in Wednesbury, Darlaston and nearby Sedgley, probably started enamelling in those places. The first recorded Wednesbury enameller was Hyla Holden, listed in the Register of Apprentices as a boxmaker in 1748, a box-painter in 1752 and as an 'enambler' in 1763. The Holden family lived in Lower High Street, Wednesbury and prospered: 'at the rear of their house there was a garden adorned with statues, fountains and stone-seated alcoves'.[2]

It is of interest to note that when Hyla Holden died in 1766 he left bequests to several members of his staff, including his mount maker and his gilder. This affirms that firstly his output was big enough for him to employ craftsmen such as these and that secondly, even though Wolverhampton and Birmingham were within easy reach, it was not necessary to

Below: A magnificent painted casket with raised panels, decorated with exotic birds and pastoral scenes taken from *The Ladies Amusement*. The two tea caddies and the sugar canister fit into velvet-lined partitions in the casket. Splendid articles such as these were made in Birmingham and in South Staffordshire and date from around 1765. The casket measures 20 cm ($7\frac{7}{8}$ ins) in length. (Victoria & Albert Museum)

obtain supplies of mounts from those places since he was completely self sufficient.

The Yardleys were a famous Wednesbury family. Samuel Yardley, who was enamelling by 1776, was succeeded by two generations of Yardleys. John Yardley was listed in a Directory of 1817 as an enamel box and toy watchmaker. These toy watches are interesting, for they were merely hollow shapes, with hands and hours painted on their dials. It was said that toy watches were bought by the miners and iron workers of the Black Country, to be worn, suspended by chains or tinned wire, with their Sunday best. But it is questionable whether, in those days of minimal pay, the labouring classes could have afforded enamel trinkets.

Moses Haughton was another Wednesbury enameller. Bernard Rackham wrote of a visit he made to Wednesbury in 1915 or 1916 when he went to see two old ladies descended from Haughton. They showed him enamels they had inherited which included several tripod salt cellars and mustard pots with small landscapes in panels on pink, green and dark blue grounds. It is known that Haughton went to Birmingham about 1764 and that he was employed there as a painter in the japanning trade. He exhibited at the Royal Academy in 1788 as an 'Enamel Painter' from Woodstock Street, Birmingham.[3] It is therefore quite possible that the enamels in question had been made in Birmingham and not in Wednesbury. Other names associated with the manufacture of enamels in this town are the families of Snape, Ross, Wilkes, Harper, and Baker. All of them contributed more than one generation to the trade.

The Trade Directory for 1783 names several manufacturers as 'Enamellers in General' and there are references to Wednesbury as a centre of enamelling in early nineteenth-century publications such as G. A. Cooke's *The Complete Itinerary of the County of Stafford* (1801), Nightingale's *Beauties of England and Wales* (1813) and Pitt's *History of Staffordshire* (1817). These references state that enamel painting in Wednesbury is of 'the highest perfection and beauty' and 'the

Right: These small, royal blue enamel boxes with thick white decoration, made around 1800, are the only type of enamels which are generally classified as Wednesbury; this is misleading since historically Wednesbury was a centre where the finest painted enamels were produced. The 'May you be happy' box measures 4 cm (1⅝ ins) in length (Halcyon Days)

84

 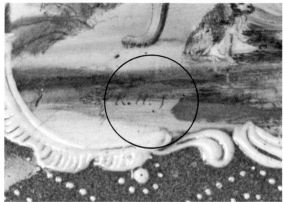

finest enamel paintings are among the productions of Wednesbury's artists.'[4]

A considerable variety of small patch-boxes were made towards the end of the eighteenth century, using the decorative technique of imposing thick white enamel on to a strong royal blue ground. This style has become particularly associated with the town of Wednesbury, to the extent that today similar boxes are invariably thus attributed. Although it is possible that some were made there, it is unfortunate that the only type of enamels to be definitely identified with so important a centre of fine production should be such simple, often crudely made, little boxes.

The extent of articles produced there can be appreciated by the variety of those recorded when the effects of John Yardley of Church Hill were dispersed in 1859. He was the grandson of Samuel Yardley and one of the last of the enamellers of South Staffordshire. His business closed in 1840. He left, among other things, enamel boxes, buttons, studs and links, plaques, medallions and small trays. F. W. Hackwood, in *Wednesbury Workshops* (1889), says the Yardley firm also made 'patch-boxes, snuff-boxes, tea caddies, salt-cellars, brooches, breast-pins for frilled shirt-fronts, door knobs and finger plates.'[5]

From this it has been assumed that all of these articles were enamelled, and undoubtedly the majority were, or at least they incorporated enamel components. Wednesbury was also a centre of metal production however, and it is by no means certain that all these objects were exclusively manufactured by the Yardley factory, as it was the custom for a manufacturer to supplement his trade by adding other firm's products to his stock.

There are few known signed or marked South Staffordshire enamels. In an age when watchmakers, goldsmiths,

Above left: *The Tea Party* engraved by Robert Hancock is one of the best known designs to have been used on English eighteenth-century ceramics. Transfer-printed in brown and overpainted, the picture is set in a panel reserved on a deep sky-blue ground with raised white scrollwork and diaper decoration. *Circa* 1765. Length 7.4 cm ($2\frac{7}{8}$ ins)

Above: This snuff-box is particularly rare as it is signed 'R.H.f.' (Robert Hancock *fecit*), as can be seen circled in this enlargement (Victoria & Albert Museum)

silversmiths and potters went to great lengths to mark their wares, it is all the more amazing that so few enamels are marked. It is possible that the principal reason that enamel paintings were so seldom signed was that they were rarely original works. That artists were irked by this tradition is revealed by the number of hidden signatures which can be found on enamels. These are usually partly obscured and can be seen only when magnified. It should be mentioned here that 'hidden signatures' are indeed rare, although in the detective eye of the keen collector every blade of grass masquerades as an initial. The name C. Davis has been found hidden in foliage on a small South Staffordshire sweetmeat dish: Robert Hancock occasionally hid his initials in an engraving and James Ross of Wednesbury, a pupil of Hancock's, did likewise. Ross, an enameller as well as an engraver, is credited with the discovery of a formula which enabled a delicate pink colour to be produced. He is said to have made a fortune by selling this much sought-after enamel.

A striking decorative effect produced in South Staffordshire is an all-over geometric pattern of white stars with red and white centres on a royal blue background. This vivid decoration was used on some of the most impressive pieces: tobacco presses, vases and chimneypiece ornaments. Another distinctive treatment was a 'gingham' finish, used principally on small boxes and trinkets. Coarse, mesh-like cambric was placed over a solid ground colour and white enamel applied on to it. When the fabric was removed, a reticulated pattern remained. Birds or sprays of flowers painted on to a gingham ground created a most appealing effect.

Raised motifs on all types of articles were achieved in two ways. One was the *repoussé* method in which the thin copper sheet was beaten into relief by means of hammering from the reverse side. An alternative technique was to build up a thick encrustation, made up of several applications of enamel on top of one another, a final coat of enamel blended smoothly with the surrounding surfaces.

In addition to these particular decorative styles, the designs of South Staffordshire enamels also incorporated rural scenes, sporting scenes and naturalistic subjects.

The attribution South Staffordshire is an umbrella term which encompasses Bilston, Wednesbury and other nearby places where enamels were produced. It is used as a designation when none of the known characteristics is present to enable a piece to be attributed to any other specific source. The reason that articles made throughout the area bore such

Below: A cassolette is an ornament with a finial which can be reversed to form a candlestick. This one is decorated in a striking all-over pattern of stars in white, red and yellow, separated by gilt motifs on a dark blue ground. South Staffordshire, *circa* 1790. Height 27.5 cm (11 in) (Victoria & Albert Museum)

close similarities was that the trade was carried on by a number of families which were closely associated. Also, in those days, every house had a workshop and most enamelling establishments adjoined the owners' homes. New designs and patterns therefore easily became common knowledge.

The dating of all of these enamels is particularly difficult since craftsmen habitually accumulate quantities of parts which they set aside to be used over the years. It is inadvisable, therefore, to date any enamel by its mount or form without taking into account the style or standard of decoration. Although a piece cannot be dated earlier than its components could have been produced, mounts and copper shapes endure and therefore might have been brought into use decades after they were made.

Among the craftsmen of South Staffordshire there have always been many who were creative as well as industrious. This applies as much today as it did 200 years ago. The enamellers of Bilston, Wednesbury and their contemporaries elsewhere provided a rapidly expanding affluent society with highly decorative personal and domestic accessories; these brought luxury and brilliant colour to Georgian candle-lit interiors.

Above: A plaque superbly painted with Watteau's *Leçon D'Amour*. A gallant is offering one of his female companions a glass of wine while they are entertained by a lute player. The painting appears to be by the same hand as the plaque on page 33. In the 1770s, when this was made, the maximum sized enamel which could be fired in the kilns then available was 20 cm (8 ins); this plaque measures 19.5 cm ($7\frac{3}{4}$ ins) in width. (Sotheby Parke Bernet & Co.)

Sadler and Green of Liverpool used a wide variety of engravings for transfer-printing on tiles; these included shipping scenes and pastoral, romantic and *chinoiserie* subjects, mostly taken from the many artistic reference books which were available during the third quarter of the eighteenth century. The majority of enamels currently attributed to Liverpool feature portraits, but it is possible that others might have been made there which are credited to Midland sources.

1 A snuff-box transfer-printed in black with two separate compartments, one for scented snuff, the other for plain. The lids are decorated with a woman and a man in theatrical costume. *Circa* 1780. Length 5.5 cm ($2\frac{1}{4}$ ins) (Wolverhampton Museum)

2 Small oval box or locket with two Liverpool enamel medallions set into a French silver mount. The medallions, which are transfer-printed in brown, show Polly Peachum and McHeath from *The Beggar's Opera* by John

Gay (1685–1732). The actress, Mrs Farrell, portrays McHeath. The transfers were taken from engravings in *Bell's British Theatre* published at the time of the revival of the opera in 1778. Height 3.3 cm ($1\frac{3}{4}$ ins) (Wolverhampton Museum)

3 A round top of a screwpeg (on which to hang hats, cloaks or swords) transfer-printed in sepia with a portrait of Admiral Hood. *Circa* 1780. Diameter 4.1 cm ($1\frac{5}{8}$ ins) (Wolverhampton Museum)

4, 5 Two round medallions, featuring a male and a female character from *The Beggar's Opera*. Diameter 4.6 cm ($1\frac{3}{4}$ ins) (Wolverhampton Museum)

6 This medallion depicts Prince William Henry (1766–1837) as a young boy of about 10 years of age; he was the third son of George III and in 1830 he became King William IV. The engraving is after a painting by Benjamin West (1738–1850). Height 7.1 cm ($2\frac{3}{4}$ ins) (Wolverhampton Museum)

7 General Sir Henry Clinton (1738–95) achieved fame following the Battle of Bunker Hill in 1775 during the American War. He played a prominent part in the capture of New York in 1776 and was promoted to Lieutenant General and knighted in the following year. Height 7.4 cm ($2\frac{7}{8}$ ins) (Halcyon Days)

8 This box is similar to many made in the Midlands, but the portrait of Augusta, Princess of Wales, the mother of George III, is comparable to others of Liverpool origin. Diameter 6.2 cm ($2\frac{1}{2}$ ins) (Wolverhampton Museum)

9 This plaque and a companion plaque of Frederick II, King of Prussia (mistakenly inscribed Frederick III), are two of the most famous Liverpool enamels. Height of unframed plaque 14.8 cm ($5\frac{7}{8}$ ins) (Halcyon Days)

The enamels on these pages are shown seven-eighths actual size.

Liverpool

Transfer-printing was the decorative
technique employed on Liverpool
enamels and one firm, Sadler and Green,
was the principal exponent of the craft.
Portraits of the famous and characters
from the theatre were among the most
popular subjects.

GEOGRAPHICALLY, Liverpool is the odd-man-out in the field of English enamels. Situated on the north-west coast, Liverpool had only one enamelling establishment. The Black Country, from Birmingham to Bilston, had at least 40, and there were many others in London, in addition to York House, Battersea.

The town has a considerable history in the field of ceramics. Delftware was made there in 1710 and by 1750 there were at least eight potteries. But, by 1780, the competition from Staffordshire had caused the number of potteries to decline to three. Liverpool potters were among the earliest to exploit transfer-printing in its own right, rather than as a short cut to decoration which gave the appearance of being hand painted.

In about 1748, John Sadler, the son of Adam Sadler, a Liverpool printer, founded, in Harrington Street, the Liverpool Printed Ware Manufactory. He was soon to be joined by Guy Green who, since a boy, had worked for Adam Sadler. The two young men, both engravers as well as printers, became partners. They claimed credit for the origination of transfer-printing, stating that they had invented it in 1749 or thereabouts and they attempted unsuccessfully to patent the process. Sadler retired in 1770 and Green continued the business until 1799.

It is significant that, on 27 July 1756, less than two months after the sale at York House, Battersea, the Liverpool partners gave a demonstration of tile printing. In an affidavit, they described how, unaided, they did:

> 'within the space of six hours, to wit betwixt the hours of nine in the morning and three in the afternoon of the same day, print upwards of twelve hundred tiles of different patterns at Liverpool . . . more in number, and better, and neater, than one hundred skilful pot painters could have painted in the like space of time in the common and usual way of painting with a pencil . . .'[1]

Although the indications are that the partners had purchased engraved copper plates and the equipment with which to print them at the Battersea sale, their claim of having been the inventors of transfer-printing was reiterated in several contemporary documents. It was also said that the idea had first occurred to Sadler as he observed some children sticking waste prints which he had given them on to broken pieces of earthenware, to make ornaments for dolls' houses.

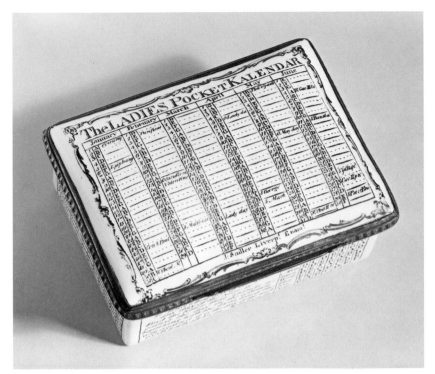

Left: An extremely rare rectangular box marked 'J. Sadler, Liverpl. Enaml.' Transfer-printed in black, it is decorated as a calendar for the years 1760–77; the lid is printed with the months January to June and the base, July to December. The inscription on the front panel gives directions how 'To find what day of the week any day of the year is.' On the back panel, there is a guide to the lunar and solar cycles. Width 8 cm (3⅛ ins) (Merseyside Museum)

On 11 February 1757, there was an advertisement in the *Liverpool Advertiser* referring to the fact that transfer-printing was being carried out in the town and concerning the proposed publication of a pamphlet by Thomas Lawrensen which would contain a description of:

> 'The new and curious art of printing or rather reprinting, from copper plates, upon porclane, enammel and earthenware, as lately practised at Chelsea, Birmingham &c.'[2]

Sadler and Green decorated not only Liverpool earthenware, but wares from other sources, as well as enamels. Wedgwood's Queen's ware used to be sent 'in the plain body' from Staffordshire, by wagon, 'for Mr Sadler's manipulation'.[3] They produced large numbers of tiles decorated with transfers which included many designs similar to those used on enamels elsewhere. Their enamels included portrait plaques of 'Frederick III, King of Prussia, Done from an original painted at Berlin in 1756', (the inscription is incorrect; the portrait is that of Frederick II—The Great) and 'The Right Honble Wm Pitt Esq., One of His Majesty's principal Secretaries of State And One of His most Honble Privy Council'. Both of these were signed 'J. Sadler, Liverp:

Right and far right: Two Liverpool oval medallions, transfer-printed in black and overpainted. A Freemason's badge, its shield charged quarterly with a lion rampant, a bull statant, a Jewish priest and an eagle displayed. The shield is supported by two cherubim; above as a crest is the Ark of the Covenant; below, around Masonic insignia, on a ribbon are the words 'Faith, Hope and Charity'.

The medallion on the right shows the arms of the Society of Bucks, a Liverpool society: two foresters support a shield painted with a stag; there is a plough and within decorative cartouches and ribbons are the inscriptions 'Freedom with Innocence—Produceth—Industry—Wealth—Be Merry and Wise'. Height 7.2 cm ($2\frac{7}{8}$ ins) (Wolverhampton Museum)

Right and far right: Two Liverpool oval enamel plaques, one with a portrait of an actor, wearing a wig, viewing himself in a hand mirror and an actress with an elaborate head-dress. Height 6.8 cm ($2\frac{5}{8}$ ins) (Wolverhampton Museum)

Enaml.' Figures of actors and actresses taken from engravings in *Bell's British Theatre* and *Bell's Shakespeare* were also used as decoration. These were published in the late 1770s and John Bell issued a series of slim volumes, one for each theatre or Shakespearean play. A print of a famous actor or actress formed the frontispiece of each book. Bell was the first printer to discard the elongated letter '*ſ*' for the simple 's'. Among additional subjects were portraits of other famous soldiers and naval heroes including General Sir Henry Clinton, Lord Cornwallis and Admirals Rodney and Hood. Two of the royal personages portrayed were Prince William Henry who was the third son of George III, and King Louis XVI of France (1754–1793) who came to the throne in 1774.

A notable Liverpool enamel is a plaque featuring *The Concert Party*. The transfer-printed design was taken from the same copper plate as that used for the frontispiece of *The Muses Delight*, engraved by James Basire, the book printed, published and sold by John Sadler in 1754. The name of another Liverpool enameller is listed in the Apprenticeship

Left: The engraving of *The Concert Party* by James Basire (1730–1802) was taken from a book entitled *The Muses Delight*, which was printed, published and sold in Liverpool in 1754 by John Sadler. Sadler and his partner, Guy Green, started printing on enamels in 1756 and so it is possible that this was among their earliest enamels. The gilt metal frame is probably the original one. Height 14.2 cm (5⅝ ins) (Wolverhampton Museum)

Indentures in the Public Record Office where it is noted that: William Rimmer of Liverpool, Enameller, took an apprentice, Edward Platt, in 1770.

Liverpool transfers on enamel are remarkable for their deep brown or black quality on a pure, cold white ground, a characteristic which is noticeable even when the print is hand coloured. It is quite possible that enamel plaques, medallions, boxes and screwpegs (on which hats, cloaks or swords could be hung) were only decorated there and that the white enamel blanks for these were obtained from other centres of enamelling.

Enamels attributable to Liverpool, other than plaques and medallions, are rare. Subjects similar to those used on Liverpool tiles appear on enamel boxes but, as most of these designs were taken from contemporary pattern books, the enamels bearing them could easily have been produced elsewhere. Out of 670 enamels displayed in an exhibition at Wolverhampton Museum in 1973, only 37, mostly plaques, were credited to Liverpool.

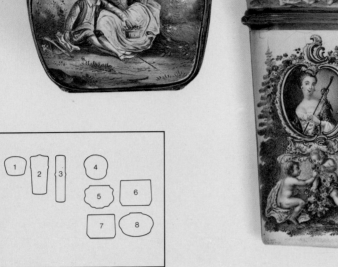

1 A view of the lid of a Viennese *bonbonnière* which is formed as a pug's head; this shows the stylized manner in which French eighteenth-century romantic scenes were painted around 1900 by Viennese enamellers. The silver-gilt mounts bear the mark of Ludwig Pollizer, who was appointed jeweller to the Shah of Persia and whose firm specialized in making small embossed toys and boxes. (Lawrence Gould Collection)

2 An enamel *étui* with silver-gilt mounts, painted in the eighteenth-century style and made in France or in Germany in the mid-nineteenth century. The yellow and purple scrolled cartouche, which frames the portrait of a lady dressed as a shepherdess, is a feature seen on English enamels, particularly those made in Birmingham around 1750–60. (Lawrence Gould Collection)

3 A German enamel bodkin case, made in the mid-nineteenth century, painted in a style similar to those made in South Staffordshire in the 1770s. (Halcyon Days)

4 A circular German enamel snuff-box of about 1740–50. The lid is painted with a scene of lovers beneath a tree, with a distant town in the background, set within a quatrefoil panel. Inside the lid is a painting of Venus with Cupid. (Lawrence Gould Collection)

5 A German enamel snuff-box, possibly made in the Fromery workshop around 1750; its French reeded silver mount has a rubbed discharge mark. The lid decoration of a musical trophy, is enamelled in green, blue and coral with encrusted gilding. The sides and base have gilt and green flowers and musical instruments. (Lawrence Gould Collection)

6 A nineteenth-century French rectangular snuff-box painted with summer flowers in the style of *Deutsche Blumen*, surrounded by borders of *bianco-sopra-bianco*

scrolling. The inside lid is painted with a scene of a lady in a park near a fountain. (Lawrence Gould Collection)

7 A Continental enamel snuff-box, possibly made in Germany in the late nineteenth century, which combines German and English eighteenth-century types of decoration. It appears that the manufacturer of this box could not decide which style to emulate. (Halcyon Days)

8 Converting the natives to Christianity—a rare eighteenth-century South German oval snuff-box. The scene painted on the lid shows a haloed priest converting savages dressed as Red Indians; the interior lid, sides and base are painted with seated sages. (Halcyon Days) The enamels illustrated on these two pages are shown actual size.

Continental Painted Enamels

Similarities existing between English and Continental copper-based enamels are apt to confuse the collector. It is vital to recognize the features which make correct attribution possible, particularly in the case of German snuff-boxes.

FROM THE fifteenth century onwards magnificent painted enamel copper-based objects were made at various times by French, German, Austrian, Swiss, Italian, Dutch, Hungarian and Spanish artist-enamellers. Naturally, an area of antiques as wide in scope as Continental enamels can only be touched on briefly here and only to the extent to which they relate to the subject of this book. It should be noted that no reference is made to miniature paintings since, although this fine work was incorporated into the decoration of many Continental copper-based vitreous enamels, the art of the miniaturist is a vast study in itself.

Of all the objects produced by European enamellers it is the snuff-box which is apt to lead to the most confusion when attributing the source of manufacture. Snuff taking by Continental and English gentlemen of the eighteenth century was an elaborate ritual in which the blend of snuff selected, the manner of taking it and above all, the number and quality of boxes owned were considered all important in assessing a man's position in society.

In eighteenth-century Europe the ubiquitous snuff-box created by enamellers, as well as an immense variety of watch cases and other elaborately decorated objects of vertu, were mostly worked in gold, often with the addition of jewelled encrustations. This is particularly true of France which was the cultural leader of the aristocratic and rich. When ostentation came to be frowned upon in France during and after the Revolution, the Swiss took over a large part of the luxury market. Enamellers in Geneva had, since the seventeenth century, been rated among the most accomplished exponents of the art of enamelling. An area in which they excelled from

Below: Two enamel snuff-boxes which were probably made by Fromery of Berlin around 1740. The smaller one has raised gilt trellis work interspersed with flowers and the silver-gilt sides are engraved with scrolling; on the silver-gilt mount is a rubbed French discharge mark. The larger box has raised gilt chevron bands with green flowers; the reeded silver mounts bear the French discharge marks of Antoine Leschaudel, Paris 1744–50. Length of the larger box 6.3 cm (2½ ins) (Lawrence Gould Collection; Halcyon Days)

the late eighteenth century was the production of elaborate, richly decorated souvenirs, often with expertly painted
lakeside scenes, and also notably the production of auto-
mated snuff-boxes. One, ordered by the Prince of Wales and
described by Horace Walpole in a letter to Mary Berry,
contained an enamelled bird which appeared on opening the
lid, sat on the rim, turned around, fluttered its wings, and
imitated various birds. It cost at the time, according to
Walpole, 'only five hundred pounds.'[1]

Although gold-based enamels were produced extensively
in Austria and in Germany, a considerable proportion of their
enamels were copper-based and similar to those made in
England. In the first half of the eighteenth century the famous
Fromery family in Berlin created exquisite, superbly decorated copper enamels. The House of Fromery was founded by
the Huguenot goldsmith, Pierre Fromery, whose son, Alexander, perfected a highly individual style of decoration which is
instantly distinguishable. It consists of a white enamel ground
with gold or silver raised decoration, occasionally interspersed with painted enamel colours, normally with green
predominating. Borders and frames of this unique type of
decoration were often used to enclose white reserves, which
bore finely painted scenes, flowers or heraldic devices. Frequently lattice-type panels were employed to all but cover the
exterior surfaces of boxes.

As the Fromerys were goldsmiths, the mounts on enamels
from their workshops were always of high quality and were
often of precious metals, although many examples with base
metal mounts exist. Lazare Duvaux, a Parisian merchant and
importer who, in 1755, was appointed 'Orfèvre-joaillier du

Above: Two German
enamel snuff-boxes dating
from about the mid-
eighteenth century. The
silver-mounted one on the
left has a lid painted with a
farmyard scene and pastoral
scenes on the base. The
shallow box on the right has
gilt-metal mounts and is a
typical example of painting
in restricted colours, which
is often seen on Continental
enamels; the base is painted
with small figures and ruins,
the only colours used being
charcoal, green and a
touch of pink. Length of
shallow box 7.5 cm (3 ins)
(Halcyon Days)

Right: A German snuff-box, of 1757–58, painted with a map of parts of Thuringia. Frederick the Great's victories between 1756 and 1757 are listed on the lid and back. Inside the lid is a painting of a Prussian soldier (the monogram FR is on his saddle cloth), his sword is poised and is about to strike two cringing Frenchmen. Width 8.5 cm (3¼ ins) (Sotheby Parke Bernet & Co.)

Roi',[2] imported Fromery enamels and mounted them in silver. This explains the fact that Fromery boxes bearing French discharge marks on their mounts are often found. Some of the finest German porcelain painters had decorated enamels for Fromery, among them the renowned Christian Friedrich Herold. He worked as an enameller in Berlin in association with the Fromery workshop until he left in 1725 to join the Meissen factory, where his speciality was the painting of harbour scenes. As one of their most esteemed and highly paid decorators, he was allowed to work as an enameller in his spare time. He continued working at Meissen until 1777. A snuff-box lid of 1739 exists signed by both Herold and Alexander Fromery. Another, in the British Museum, is signed '*Herold fecit*'. His typical style on enamels shows figures in gilded relief against a painted background.

Dresden, the great centre of porcelain production, was also the source of a considerable output of exceedingly fine enamels. In many instances, as with Herold, the same artist's work can be found on porcelain and on enamels. It was the custom for factories to send out blanks to be decorated by painters working independently either in studios set up for this purpose, or in their own homes. These artists were known as *Hausmalerei*. Attempts at producing the Fromery distinctive style of enamelling were made elsewhere. Examples of some Russian eighteenth-century enamels indicate the possibility that Fromery-trained German enamellers were at work in Moscow. Peter the Great and the Empress Catherine were both anxious to encourage the crafts and recruited many skilled workmen from abroad. However, compared to the vast quantities of enamelled objects of vertu which were produced in most European countries in the eighteenth century, comparatively few appear to have originated in Russia. There, the silversmith reigned supreme and niello work was highly esteemed until the end of the nineteenth century. In Russia, a middle class, such as there was in England, did not exist. Although the court and the aristocracy in England set the fashion for enamels, it was the middle class that created the mass market for them.

Danish enamel boxes produced in Copenhagen around 1760 imitated those made in porcelain some two decades earlier at Mennecy in France and at the Du Paquier factory in Vienna. These were often shallow oblong boxes, either painted in *trompe l'oeil* fashion to simulate envelopes, which sometimes bore amatory inscriptions, or left decorated with playing cards, crudely drawn maps or stanzas from popular songs. In contrast, finely painted portraits appeared inside the lids. Similarly decorated enamel boxes were also made in Germany, in England, and occasionally in Russia.

Although high-quality hand-painted German and Austrian enamel-on-copper boxes were still being produced in the second half of the eighteenth century, some made during the period of Prussia's Seven Year's War (1757–63) were merely inferior propaganda pieces. Objects commemorating Frederick the Great's battles were quickly painted in order to be made available to the public while the news was still hot, one being dated within a week of the Battle of Leuthen on 5 December 1757.

Many English as well as Continental Frederick the Great snuff-boxes exist to this day. His portrait, his battle scenes or their dates, his monogram and adulatory inscriptions were the sycophantic motifs the decorators chose. Some boxes of this period have been ascribed to Daniel Chodowiecki, Frederick's chief designer and engraver. It is said that although the warrior king owned some fifteen hundred snuff-boxes, he adopted the messy habit of keeping snuff loose in a special pocket in his uniform.

In eighteenth-century Vienna, the enamelling workshops of the von Jungers flourished from about 1764 to 1780. There were two brothers, Christoph, who died in 1777, and Johann, who continued the factory until his death in 1790. Their range of products was extensive and included domestic articles such as jugs and coffee pots, with decoration imitative of the Sèvres porcelain which was so fashionable at that time. These found favour with the ruling classes of the Ottoman Empire and *zarfs* (Turkish coffee cups) were made by von Jungers for this market.

Up to the mid-nineteenth century a certain elegance of style was attempted in the manufacture of Viennese enamels. Works by great artists, such as the battle scenes of Wouwerman and classical subjects reminiscent of Rubens, were often the inspiration for ambitious decorators. Generally, Viennese nineteenth-century caskets, ewers, clocks, musical boxes and other objects were a pastiche of Renaissance or eighteenth-century romantic designs. Many of these were made to be passed off as the genuine article and, although great skill went into their manufacture, the results were rarely successful.

From the late 1890s until 1914, the firm of Brüder, Gottlieb und Brauchbar of Brunn in Austria (now Brno, Czechoslovakia) produced enamelled steel beakers and mugs to commemorate special, principally royal, occasions in many countries including Russia and England. These were decorated with transfer-printed designs, usually florid in character and often in bizarre colours. The portraits of the heroes of the day were frequently reproduced from photographs. Similar beakers were made in Germany.

Around 1920, the Vienna School of Arts and Crafts influenced a modernistic revival. Enamels were decorated with machine-like precision to create geometric and Tyrolean-type patterns on small household articles such as ash-trays and bowls and on jewellery. More recently, many of these designs have incorporated brightly coloured artificial gemstones, which are vulgar in the extreme. A profusion of enamel souvenirs totally lacking in artistic merit has also been produced in Vienna in recent times: miniature Louis XV style furniture with enamel panels decorated with crude colour transfers set in cheap ormolu frames typify these tasteless articles.

In France, the goldsmith reigned supreme and there was limited production of copper enamels in the eighteenth and early nineteenth centuries. In the 1840s, a revival of Limoges enamel started at Sèvres. From then until the 1890s this style of enamelling enjoyed extreme popularity and in Paris there were several workshops making replicas of Limoges artefacts. The revival was at its height in the late 1880s when three major exhibitions of this work were held in France and in Germany.

In addition to limited production of somewhat traditional

enamel designs featuring flowers, romantic or genre subjects and apart from the fakes produced by the firm of Samson, a particular type of trinket box and jewel casket continued to be made in France from the mid-nineteenth century until the beginning of the 1914–18 war. These had elaborately cast and chased ormolu frames into which were set panels enamelled on copper, usually with floral motifs (lily-of-the-valley was a great favourite) surrounded by borders of encrusted opalescent enamel beads, imitative of Sèvres porcelain. These boxes were usually lined with deeply buttoned satin or velvet.

Apart from the distinctive types already described, many eighteenth- and early nineteenth-century Continental painted copper enamels bear such close resemblance to those made at the same time in England that on some occasions it is difficult for all but the expert to distinguish one from the other. Some Continental boxes, sealing wax cases, dishes and other small items are heavier than their English counterparts, having been made from a thicker gauge of copper. Others, which are delicately painted, employ varying tones of very few colours instead of a full palette, to portray elaborate floral designs or landscapes. The shapes of some Continental enamels are often quite unlike similar objects of English manufacture; it is only by closely observing and comparing both types that the differences, which might only be subtle ones, become obvious.

Fakes, Forgeries and Replicas

From the 1850s English eighteenth-century enamels were superbly reproduced, but even the best examples can be identified as copies.

Left: A group of fakes and replicas, all made by Samson of Paris with the exception of number 3, which is a German late nineteenth-century copy of an eighteenth-century box painted with stag hunting scenes. The other articles emulate English enamels of Midland origin. It is not possible to date exactly the enamels made by Samson but better quality ones, such as numbers 6 and 7, were made about 1890. The small Wrestling and the Windsor Castle boxes (numbers 4 and 5) might have been produced as late as the 1960s. This type of English box was usually transfer-printed whereas these fakes are hand-painted. Numbers 1, 2 and 8 are typical Samson reproductions of elaborate South Staffordshire enamels. (no. 4, Wolverhampton Museum; no. 5, Lawrence Gould Collection, others, Private Collection) Shown actual size.

Above left: a superb tea caddy from the Schreiber Collection at the Victoria and Albert Museum. It is a perfect example of an enamel decorated with engravings from the book, *The Ladies Amusement,* published around 1760. The exotic birds are copied from a design by C. Fenn, engraved by P. Benazech; the festoons and sprays of flowers are after designs by J. P. Pillement engraved by C. H. Hemerich. Width 11 cm (4 ins) It was ambitious for Samson to copy this elegant piece and he did so with only limited success, as seen above. Compare the painting and note that Samson's birds and trees are too large. The shape of the copy is also inferior to the original and its ormolu handle is too small. (Victoria & Albert Museum; Private Collection)

Fake, forgery or merely reproduction: are these the sincerest forms of flattery? A fake is a 'trick or invention', thus a stylistic imitation but not a copy, and a forgery is 'the making of a thing in fraudulent imitation', a copy designed to deceive.[1] Nowhere are the demarcation lines more blurred than in the study of ceramics. To quote from Otto Kurz's book called *Fakes*:

> 'In the field of European ceramics of the eighteenth century everything was imitated by everybody, and beginning from the fact that the whole of the European china manufacture is an open attempt at faking Chinese porcelain the whole history of the craft is a series of mutual betrayals of professional secrets and of the wholesale stealing of ideas and inventions. As soon as one factory, be it Meissen, Sèvres, or Wedgwood, produced a novel and successful shape or colour scheme, it was pirated by as many factories as wanted to partake in its success. . . Nor did these habits change with the nineteenth century; the imitation of everything, old and new, remaining as usual as ever.'[2]

A piece of Worcester porcelain with blue under-glaze decoration, to which elaborate over-glaze decoration in full colours has been added, is an obvious forgery. A piece of 'Sèvres' china with a date-mark for 1760, made out of hard paste porcelain, is of course a fake. But in respect of enamels, which were almost never marked, the copy is much more difficult to discern. In the case of copies of ornate 1770s pieces (many of which were themselves near copies of Sèvres and Meissen porcelain) the elaborate shapes, flamboyant colours and gilded enrichments were facets which the forgers were adept at emulating. But what they took less trouble over or perhaps were incapable of reproducing was the fine draughtsmanship and delicate painting of the scenes and flowers, many of which compared favourably with the best works of contemporary miniaturists. When objects of simple shape and restrained decoration were copied one questions why the copier did not go to the little extra trouble required to do a better job. The most copied of all were small patch-boxes and snuff-boxes which were reproduced in vast quantities.

The first replicas of English eighteenth-century enamels appeared for sale on the Continent around the 1850s. The most famous copier of ceramics of all time was the firm of Samson of Paris, but this was by no means the only nine-

Below: This *étui* by Samson of Paris is a fake in the true sense of the word. It is copied from one made in South Staffordshire in the 1770s, every feature being duplicated, including the raised gilt rococo scrolling and the style of the chased gilt metal mounts. But the delicate quality of the original is absent and the painting is noticeably inferior. Made by Samson around 1900. Height 9.5 cm (3¾ ins) (Private Collection)

teenth-century maker of 'reproductions'. Many others reproduced—or faked, depending on their motives—the popular *objets d'art* of the day. The quality of some of the work would be the envy of manufacturers today. Samson products are collectors' items in their own right, although they fetch only a fraction, albeit a large fraction, of the price of their eighteenth-century prototypes.

Among scores of other objects, many of them as yet unidentified, Samson made splendid English-style enamels, which were a source of pride to the firm and much sought-after by the *nouveau riche* looking for imitations of the delightful boxes and *bibelots* enjoyed by the élite. The aristocracy also patronized the famous firm when they needed expert replacements for broken items in their Chinese Lowestoft or Meissen dinner services, or when lids needed replacing on their expensive enamel snuff-boxes.

The House of Samson was founded in 1845 by Edmé Samson in Rue Beranger, Paris, and specialized in decorating china. It was Edmé's son, Emile, who began to reproduce early porcelains, earthenware and enamels. His son, Léon, succeeded on Emile's death in 1913 and in 1923 the great grandson of Edmé took over the business. In recent years the firm has been owned by Christian Richardier and now operates from Rue de la Révolution, Montreuil, France.

Following the 1862 Special Exhibition of Works of Art at the South Kensington Museum (now the Victoria and Albert Museum), well-to-do Victorian merchants who were able to view collections made by the nobility, began demanding the same things, or copies, for themselves. For this market, Samson produced innumerable replicas or impressions of eighteenth-century English enamel plaques, boxes, and *bonbonnières*, as well as versions of Meissen, Chelsea, Worcester, Bow, Derby, French faience and porcelain, Chinese armorial wares and other types of ceramics. In 1930 the Samson

Below: Enlargements of scenes on two boxes: right, a pastoral scene on an original Bilston enamel; left, the same picture, interpreted by Samson. Scenes within panels on the sides of the original box have also been duplicated onto the copy, which is coarser in every feature. Although the painting is inferior, the enamelling is of a high standard on this 'early' Samson, made around 1870. (Halcyon Days)

letter-head enumerated nearly 50 kinds of reproductions. Their showrooms resembled a small museum with entire rooms devoted to specific periods or types of artefacts.

It is extremely likely that Emile Samson and his successors would have been happy and proud to sign most of their products so that there would be no mistaking the talents responsible. But, above all, Emile Samson was an astute businessman who knew full well that his customers would not stand for it. Samson's aim was to make products of such quality that they would be indistinguishable from originals. However, a good many items were in fact marked and the marks were often removed by succeeding owners. The firm's most used mark was the crossed S, but a series of fake marks on porcelain representing the crossed swords of Meissen, the red anchor of Chelsea, as well as others were also employed.

The Samson firm excelled in quality as well as quantity and among their most successful lines were copies of English enamels from the 1770–80 period. The majority of these were produced in the early years of the 1900s when a vogue existed for the charming and tasteful toys enjoyed by the Georgian élite. While the specialist may be able to tell from the 'feel' of an enamel that it is not the same as the original or that the hinge and metal mount are not nearly so well made, less experienced collectors may be forgiven for failing to recognize unmarked painted enamels as fakes. A give-away feature on the majority of small Samson boxes is a central protruding lug on the outside hinge which acts as a stop to prevent the lid opening backwards too far. This lug is not present on the superior quality, patterned mounts used by Samson on larger pieces. Another detail to look for on Samson boxes is a finely milled finish to the mounts, a ribbed pattern obviously machined on the outermost edge.

The excellence of the best work can be judged by the fact that two Samson large oval boxes in the Bilston Museum collection were, until 1973, catalogued as Birmingham *c.* 1770. These had lobed edges, and were decorated with Mediterranean harbour scenes. Samson did not use transfer-prints as the firm's pride was in being able to imitate pretty eighteenth-century scenes painted free-hand. Even when they copied transfer-printed designs on small patch-boxes, these were also painted by hand. Their finest reproductions included tea caddies and candlesticks with richly coloured and embellished backgrounds. One of the most frequently faked of all enamel articles was the bottle ticket or decanter label. Although Samson produced these in wholesale quantities, they were also reproduced in many countries.

The production of Samson enamels ceased when the company found that hand-painted enamels which required intricate hinged mounts were no longer a profitable proposition. For some years there had been a diminishing demand for the artistically impoverished designs they had been producing. These looked the inferior copies they were and the *antiquaires* who had been their principal customers were no longer prepared to pay the high prices Samson were forced to ask. In 1975, a London antique dealer purchased the remnants of Samson's enamelling department for their curiosity value: ancient press-tools and moulds, box bases and lids which did not match each other, copper blanks intended for decanter labels and plaques. Significantly, there were no

Left: Two nineteenth-century boxes by Samson. The one on the left is a copy of an eighteenth-century Birmingham box, painted with a river scene; that on the right is copied from a German early nineteenth-century box. Both boxes bear Samson's marks which are shown enlarged below.
The bottom illustration is a close-up of a hinge which is typical of those used on many Samson boxes, showing the central protruding 'lug'; this lug is not seen on the hinges of English eighteenth-century boxes.
(Wolverhampton Museum; Lawrence Gould Collection)

mounts as these had always been made by sub-contractors and the difficulty and high cost of obtaining them was a further contributory factor in the decision to close down the firm's enamelling department.

In Vienna, copies of Renaissance enamels were made from the 1770s until the 1914–18 war, the firm of Hermann Ratzerdorfer being one of the leading manufacturers during the late nineteenth century. Prolific quantities of Limoges-style enamels were produced from the 1840s onwards in France, the revival at Sèvres setting the trend for others to follow. Julien Robillard of Paris was one of the most successful manufacturers in this field and later in the century and until the early 1900s, Samson, too, faked Limoges enamels. Although fakes were highly profitable, much of the production at this time in Vienna and in Paris was the result of a genuine desire to resurrect past techniques which had never been surpassed.

A faker of antiquities who operated at the very highest level was Salomon Weininger, born in Hungary in 1822. He

became an antique dealer in Vienna and was entrusted to restore famous Renaissance works of art, most of which incorporated enamelling, from the Geistliche Schatzkammer (Spiritual Treasury) of the Holy Roman Empire. His system was to make copies, return them to the museum and to sell the originals for vast sums to other museums or to very rich collectors. As a result of these activities, he ended his days in the Austrian State Prison, where he died in 1879.

It was about 1867 that one of the most famous of English collectors, Lady Charlotte Schreiber, began to amass a large collection of precious items, including English enamels. On a visit to Madrid in 1878, Lady Charlotte bought a pair of 'eighteenth-century' vases which she later showed to Emile Samson in Paris. It must have been with glee that he was able to prove to her that they had been made in his workshops.

Antique dealers and collectors are constantly on their guard against fakes. These are usually fed into the market discreetly and it is a shock when an important piece is discovered to be one. Occasionally however, articles appear which within their class are so spectacular they at once become suspect.

Into this category can be placed a series of very large enamel plaques which have been sold through Sotheby's on different occasions in recent years, clearly and correctly catalogued as 'Continental, late 19th century'. Their subjects, nevertheless, were views of eighteenth-century London: St James's Park, Wauxhall [sic] Gardens, Kew, Clapham and Lambert [sic] Bridge. London scenes such as these frequently figured on eighteenth-century prints, but rarely on enamels. The plaques were clearly signed 'JFK, 1770' and the reverse bore a paper label inscribed in ink: 'This pair of Enamel plaques was given to Lady Janssen by the Painter J. F. Knight as a token of gratitude for her constant patronage while he was employed at the Battersea Works'. There is no record of a 'J. F. Knight' having been an enamel painter at Battersea or anywhere else. Apart from all of these unlikely features, their size, almost 35 centimetres (14 inches) wide, confirmed that they were certainly not authentic. Eighteenth-century enamel plaques were usually quite small. The famous 'Success to the British Fishery' plaque measured less than 13 centimetres (5 inches) across, and the important Birmingham plaques which were set into japanned caskets were generally not more than approximately 18 centimetres (7 inches) wide. Large enamel plaques were painted by a London artist, William Hopkins Craft. But the size of his works, which included portraits of the famous, was exceptional.

In the British Museum there is a large oval plaque by Craft; it is painted with a rustic scene in the style of Boucher and measures 38 centimetres (15 inches) in height. At the turn of the nineteenth century there was a market for ostentatious pieces of indifferent quality such as the plaques with London views. A classic example of supply meeting demand.

There will always be imposters in every sphere of life, particularly in the world of fine art, and in 1978 fakes of English enamels are still being made and fed into the market, apparently in small numbers. Boxes similar to those illustrated can occasionally be seen in so-called antique shops; they are crude in the extreme and would delude only the most inexperienced purchaser. The author is not aware of any mid-twentieth century fakes of elaborate English enamels. To reproduce perfectly the constituent parts of ornate eighteenth-century enamel objects, and then to decorate them to a standard which connoisseurs might acknowledge as originals, would be very costly.

Below: A group of present day fakes, shown actual size. The painted decoration is extremely coarse, the shapes are crude and the mounts have been aged with chemicals. These can occasionally be seen on sale as 'genuine English eighteenth-century enamels'. (Private Collection)

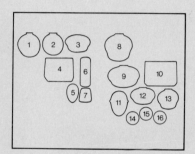

1 'A Token of Friendship', a box produced in June 1970. This was the first contemporary enamel on which attempts at hand colouring were made; prior to this, all decoration had been in monochrome. The protruding hinge was the best that could then be obtained in the comparatively small numbers required. Today, contemporary Bilston hinged mounts compare favourably with those on eighteenth-century boxes.

2 Halcyon is the Greek name for the kingfisher. There is a legend that, during the ten days around the winter solstice, the bird laid its eggs in a nest floating on the Aegean Sea and so charmed the waves that the eggs were hatched on a tranquil sea, beneath cloudless blue skies. These are the Halcyon Days; they signify peace and happiness.

3 An oval box decorated with an eighteenth-century shooting scene.

4 A limited edition box featuring the Victoria and Albert Museum; on the sides are scenes of Kensington Palace, the Round Pond in Kensington Gardens, Egerton Crescent and Kynance Mews.

5 Birds and foliage on a miniature egg-shaped box.

6, 7 A needlecase and a thimble, decorated with pink roses.

8 The game of polo, introduced into England in 1875, is featured on this circular box.

9 The Mozart Box from 'The Great Classical Composers' collection. The preceding box in the collection, issued in 1970, commemorated the bicentenary of the birth of Beethoven and was the first limited edition of the revival. The succeeding boxes depicted Bach, Handel and Haydn.

10 The Johann Strauss box was made in 1975 to commemorate the 150th anniversary of the birth of the composer. It is inscribed: 'It is no small thing to have played for Mankind to dance.'

11 This egg-shaped box is inscribed, 'Do think of me when this you see tho' many miles we distant be'.

12 An oval box inscribed 'Happiness is the thing that makes you feel that Now is the best time of the year'.

13 A vividly hand-coloured design of wild flowers on a royal blue base.

14, 15, 16 Three miniature boxes decorated with hand-coloured transfer-prints. The enamels illustrated on these two pages are shown actual size. (Halcyon Days)

Decline and Revival of a Craft

By the 1830s the fashion for elegant
English enamels had passed. In 1970 a
Mayfair antique shop together with a small
firm in Bilston brought about a rebirth
of traditional English enamelling skills.

I T IS, PERHAPS, somewhat surprising that the craft of making these popular enamel trifles should have died out. Their success during the last decades of the eighteenth century had been phenomenal and they were exported to countries all over the world, including Russia and Colonial America. The business which the Birmingham and South Staffordshire enamellers did with France was important enough to cause Napoleon specifically to ban their products; about the same time duty was imposed on them by Prussia. By the early 1800s enamellers were turning their hands to other things. With the Industrial Revolution escalating and the Napoleonic Wars causing economic difficulties for small businesses in England, there was a sustained shift of labour to the big new factories. Production of iron and steel became more profitable than hand-crafts and the hazard to health of working with ingredients which contained high proportions of lead, mercury and arsenic—often in foul, unventilated workshops—added to the desire for a change of employment on the part of the enamellers in the South Midlands.

In London, long before the turn of the eighteenth century, it would seem that enamellers found that the toys they were producing had lost their charm. Having been greeted with brio when they were a new fad, they would certainly have been rejected by the *haut monde* when they became commonplace.

Another factor in the decline of enamelling was the diminishing demand for snuff-boxes, which had been one of the principal products of the industry. The habit of snuff-taking which thrived from the 1700s was most popular from about 1750–85, coinciding with the great period for enamels.

In France, under Louis XV, snuff played so important a part that the period was called the *Siècle de la Tabatière*. In England some of the most famous people in the land took up the habit, among them Beau Nash and Dr Johnson. Queen Charlotte, wife of George III, was so addicted that she became known as Snuffy Charlotte. But during the last quarter of the eighteenth century, cigarettes were introduced. In 1804, the German playwright Kotzebue wrote that in Paris 'to take snuff is getting rather out of fashion, while smoking is coming into vogue in its stead'.[1]

The change in taste brought about by the progressing influence of neoclassicism had resulted in the rejection of pretty enamel *bibelots* with their emphasis on rococo motifs and brightly coloured subject matter. In the closing years of the eighteenth century, sombre Etruscan hues became the most stylish and these did not lend themselves to English

Left: The Royal Yacht Britannia box was commissioned by Her Majesty, Queen Elizabeth II on the occasion of the Royal State visit to the United States of America for the 1976 Bicentennial celebrations. The Queen's cypher is enamelled inside the base within a cartouche. The oval box has a *bombé* base, enamelled in royal blue, and a hand-chased gold-plated mount; drawing by Rodney Shakell. Length 7.3 cm (2⅞ ins) (Reproduced by gracious permission of Her Majesty the Queen. Copyright reserved)

enamel designs. Their era as expensive toys was over by the first decades of the nineteenth century.

During the Art Nouveau period a few artists used painted enamels for some of their designs but it was not until 1970 that the eighteenth-century English craft of making fine enamel objects was revived.

Halcyon Days, situated in London's Brook Street and established since 1950 as one of the few antique shops to specialize in eighteenth-century English enamels, had sought for some years to bring about a revival of the craft. Antique enamels had become increasingly scarce as the fashion to collect them had gathered momentum during the 1960s. They had never been produced in quantities as great as most other antiques since the entire life span of the industry which created them had been less than a hundred years. The china, pottery and glass industries only developed into real mass-production in the 1840s, just after enamelling had declined and ceased.

In December 1968, the author, a director of Halcyon Days, was introduced to Kenneth Marshall, his son Ian and his son-in-law, Neal Hughes, by Kenneth West, one of Birmingham's leading silversmiths. Their factory in Bilston manufactured enamel powder for industrial purposes, principally for the enamelling of cookers and refrigerators. All three men had studied enamelling and they had set up a small laboratory within the factory to experiment with the techniques employed two centuries earlier by their predecessors, whose decorative enamels had brought fame to Bilston.

The partners had formed a company called Copper

Enamels and they were beginning to manufacture articles of contemporary design—vases, napkin rings, candlesticks and ashtrays, enamelled in solid, brilliant colours. The high standard of craftsmanship so impressed the author that she suggested a change of direction towards a more imaginative design policy.

Instead of producing domestic articles in plain colours she visualized the potential of making precious hand-decorated enamels, particularly small boxes, in the spirit of the eighteenth century, and proposed a joint venture. Halcyon Days' experience of the international antique business, and their specialized knowledge of Georgian design would combine with Copper Enamels' technical expertise to create a whole new world of collectors' items, the aim being to bring about an authentic revival of an eighteenth-century craft. This objective was particularly appropriate in view of Bilston's history as one of the great traditional English centres of enamelling.

Within a short time, a close working relationship was formed between the two companies and a trade-name chosen—Bilston and Battersea Enamels. The artistic achievements associated with these names had provided the inspiration for the revival and the directors believed that, if the enamels were marketed under this name, an instant awareness of their

Right: In 1973, the first dated contemporary Bilston enamel Easter egg was made. This was followed in subsequent years by other dated boxes made for Christmas, St Valentine's Day and Mother's Day. In 1977 the first Bilston Year box was issued; 'A Year to Remember' was inscribed inside the lid. These editions are produced only for limited periods and the date when production will cease is announced in advance. Size of egg-shaped box, 4.2 cm (1⅝ ins) in diameters. (Halcyon Days)

history would be evoked in the minds of potential collectors and export buyers.

All those involved in the design and manufacturing processes have experienced the satisfaction which comes from creating an article of quality and beauty. Artists are delighted to see their drawings lovingly interpreted with elegance and charm, and those who give, receive and collect contemporary Bilston enamels regard them with great affection.

During the early days of the enterprise tremendous problems had to be overcome. It was essential to recruit and train a work force to master the intricate skills of an earlier age and at the same time produce a selection of enamels to test the market. Following the production of satisfactory prototypes, one of the difficulties which had to be faced was that only small quantities of metal components were required. In twentieth-century Birmingham, metal parts, tooled to precise specifications, had to be ordered in thousands to justify high origination costs. Having parts made by hand as an alternative was far too expensive. Prior to mid-1970, it was not known, of course, whether the revival would be well received. Even if successful, it would be possible to plan only in terms of hundreds for processing entirely by hand. Much time was lost before sympathetic manufacturers, with faith in the project, could be found to supply components in the relatively small numbers required. The copper shapes were, and still are, made by Brian Edmonds of Birmingham, who has

Above: 1 A box issued in 1971 for the St Paul's Cathedral Appeal; drawing by Geoffrey Fletcher.
2 The Churchill Centenary Trust commissioned this box in 1974 to mark the centenary of Sir Winston Churchill's birth; drawings by Eric Thomas.
3 A box to commemorate the Royal State Visit to the United States of America in July 1976; the portraits are by Molly Bishop. The sides are decorated with the Union Flag and Old Glory, surrounded by the flags of the first 13 States to sign the Declaration of Independence.
4 A box which commemorated the Silver Jubilee of Queen Elizabeth II in 1977. A picture of the State Coach returning to Buckingham Palace after the Coronation is on the lid and around the sides are views of Windsor Castle, Balmoral Castle, the Palace of Holyrood House and Sandringham House. This box measures 7.3 cm ($2\frac{7}{8}$ ins) (Halcyon Days)

enthusiastically supported the enterprise. Kenneth West and his son, Russell, have devoted their time and great skill to perfect the hinged mounts which they produce; these now compare favourably with mounts on antique enamel boxes.

A family friend of the directors of Copper Enamels was Tony Wylde, an experienced artist-enameller whose advice on enamelling procedures proved invaluable. Wylde was also an accomplished artist whose drawings of Black Country scenes are well-known. He was the first to execute drawings for the ceramic lithographs which were used to transfer patterns to the enamels prior to hand painting.

Ceramic lithographs are the contemporary equivalent of transfer-prints. Today the kilns in which enamels are fired are heated by electricity instead of coal. Apart from these two modern developments, Bilston and Battersea Enamels are subjected to the same multiple hand-applied processes as were their eighteenth-century counterparts.

During the first few months of 1970, only samples were produced and these were not marked. But a trade-mark was soon devised and, since production got under way in July of that year, everything made by the factory has borne a distinctive mark.

It was decided as a matter of policy to commission original drawings from talented artists, rather than to reproduce old

Right: Lion Flower was created by artist Fleur Cowles for an edition which was issued jointly in the United Kingdom and the United States by Halcyon Days and the Horchow Collection, Dallas.
Far right: In 1976, the Horchow Collection commissioned a series of boxes on behalf of the American Institute for Public Service and the first box featured George Washington; drawing by Ian Adam. Diameter 6 cm (2⅜ ins).
Right: Two boxes commissioned by Cartier, New York, for whom they are made exclusively. The Cartier logo is incorporated into the design of a game of backgammon; drawing by Frederick Baylis.
The oval box has *chinoiserie* scenes taken from *The Ladies Amusement*; drawings by Ian Adam. Width 7.3 cm (2 ins). (Horchow Collection; Cartier, New York)

patterns. For motto boxes, however, the sentiments expressed in the eighteenth-century could not in some cases be bettered, but the calligraphy and the decoration for the new designs is in every case originated by Halycon Days, never copied from an antique.

Collectors of enamels do not appear to have changed in the past two hundred years, and their preference for traditional subjects is reflected in many of the designs chosen for contemporary Bilston enamels: flowers, birds, animals, romantic themes, sporting pastimes, seascapes, pastoral scenes, famous buildings, portraits and emblems. Occasionally the work of several artists is combined in the decoration of a box, each making their individual contribution to the design. Rectangular boxes have eight surfaces which can be decorated; one artist might create the principal drawings for the lid, the panels around the base and the interior of the box, another the decorative frames, and a calligrapher the inscriptions.

Many famous artists have been commissioned to create designs, among them Molly Bishop, Fleur Cowles, Moira Hoddell, Geoffrey Fletcher, and Dennis Flanders. Boxes have been produced for a variety of events and organizations: The St Paul's Cathedral Appeal, The Churchill Centenary Trust, The National Trust of Australia, The World Wildlife Fund, The City of Amsterdam's 700th Anniversary, The Aldeburgh Festival's 25th Anniversary, for Cartier, New York, and special commissions have been executed for overseas governments and museums.

The small enamel box is a perfect medium on which to record events of note. Since 1975, special boxes have been made to mark the Bicentenary of the United States of America, the Silver Jubilee of Her Majesty Queen Elizabeth II, and centenaries as diverse as the Wimbledon Tennis Tournament, the St John Ambulance Association and the first performance of Tchaikovsky's ballet *Swan Lake*. Dated boxes are issued annually for St Valentine's Day, Mother's Day, Easter and Christmas. These editions emulate one of the original purposes for which their eighteenth-century counterparts were produced, the commemoration of important occasions.

Today, in 1978, it is only eight years since the revival in Bilston began, but considerable progress has already been made. A highly skilled team of men and women now produce over 120 different designs. The range includes boxes in 24 different shapes and sizes, thimbles, needlecases, photograph frames, beakers, musical boxes and carriage clocks, the majority being exported throughout the world.

All contemporary Bilston enamels are marked. The mark shown at the top is currently in use and has appeared on enamels produced since 1980. The centre mark was in use from 1970 to 1980; the lower one was used for special commissions from 1970-1973.

Collecting

The variety of English enamel objects is fascinating—they are among the most intriguing and colourful collectors' items in the world.

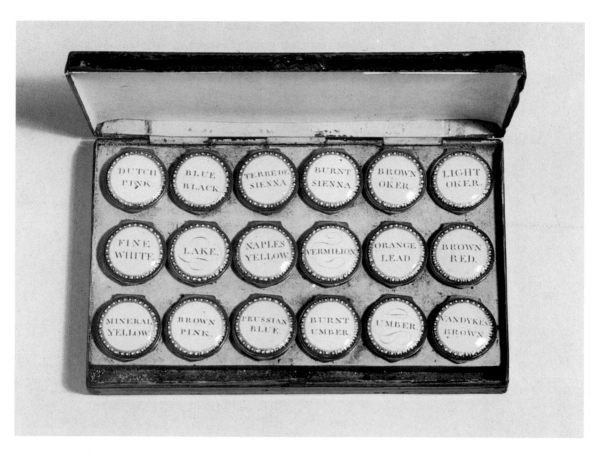

Left: A group of enamels illustrating some of the objects made in England between 1770 and 1800.

1 A quadrille poole or counter tray; quadrille was a popular card game in the eighteenth century. Trays such as this were sold in sets of five, one for each player, and one for the kitty; they are generally attributed to Bilston.

2 A Bilston *étui* containing a small glass scent bottle.

3 A view of the back of an enamel and gilt metal verge watch, no. 758, by William Aukland of London, *circa* 1760.

4 This tiny basket-shaped box was probably made in Birmingham and might have hung from a châtelaine.

5, 6 Eighteenth-century enamel thimbles and tape measures are rare and much sought-after; the tape measure has raised white decoration on a 'gingham' background. Bilston *circa* 1780.

7 *Bonbonnières* such as this, in the form of a very small apple, are among the most attractive South Staffordshire toys.

8 An inkpot and quill stand combined, the lid painted *en trompe l'oeil*, the base with bouquets and sprays of summer flowers—Birmingham or London. *Circa* 1765. The enamels on the facing page are shown actual size. (Halcyon Days)

Above: A very rare, possibly unique, set of 18 enamel boxes containing artist's colours in the original japanned metal case. South Staffordshire or Birmingham *circa* 1800. Width of case 9.8 cm (7⅝ ins) (Lawrence Gould Collection)

THE DOYENNE of English collectors of eighteenth-century *objets d'art* was Lady Charlotte Schreiber, daughter of the ninth Earl of Lindsay. She was an accomplished etcher, she played the harp and as a girl learnt French, German, Italian, Persian, Greek, Hebrew and Latin. In her antique collecting years, these languages were a great asset. As the wife of Sir Josiah John Guest, her first husband, the world's greatest iron-master, she mixed in a brilliant circle. Among her friends were Tennyson, Disraeli, Ruskin and the Duke of Wellington. In 1853 at the age of 40, she was left an immensely rich widow. Three years later she married the tutor to the eldest of her 10 children, Charles Schreiber, a Suffolk gentleman and Fellow of Trinity College, Cambridge, who was 14 years her junior.

From about 1867, for some 15 years, the Schreibers travelled the continent of Europe in a fervent, unceasing quest for antique treasures. Lady Charlotte referred to these tours as

Right: English enamels were extensively exported and the enamellers were quick to exploit events which could be commemorated on boxes and on plaques. General Washington was Commander-in-Chief of the American army during the War of Independence and became the first President of the United States in 1789. It was probably about 1785 that this plaque was made in Birmingham or in South Staffordshire. The General is painted wearing a dark blue uniform with yellow and gold epaulettes, his powdered hair *en queue*. Height 9.8 cm (3⅞ ins) (John C. Walsh Collection)

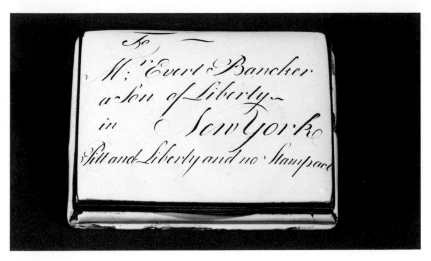

chasses and, at the end of each day, details of every transaction were recorded with enthusiasm. Her son, Montague Guest, wrote of her:

> 'She hunted high and low, through England and abroad; France, Holland, Germany, Spain, Italy, Turkey, all were ransacked; she left no stone unturned, no difficulty, discomfort, fatigue or hardship of travel daunted her, or turned her from her purpose, and she would come back, after weeks on the Continent, to Langham House, Portland Place, where she lived, rich with the fruits of her expeditions.'[1]

Her collection was unique both in its magnitude and quality; it included lace, fans, playing cards, prints, pottery, glass and enamels. The journals, which she wrote describing her travels and purchases, reveal a woman of great good taste, a pioneer in the appreciation of English *objets d'art* and one who kept a tight grip on her expenditures.

No matter how wonderful the item, if, in her estimation, the price was not right, she would not buy. From the following information, which is extracted from her records of a trip to Italy in 1869, it is clear that the amounts she paid for enamels rarely exceeded £2 on a single purchase. She bought a snuffbox in the form of a bird for £1.10s, a small enamel head for 1s.6d. and two coloured enamel pegs for 4s. She also bought a pair of Battersea candlesticks identical to a pair she had previously rejected for £20 except that the latter were in perfect condition whereas the former were 'a good bit injured in the sunk part in the base', and cost £2.[2] She rejected a very

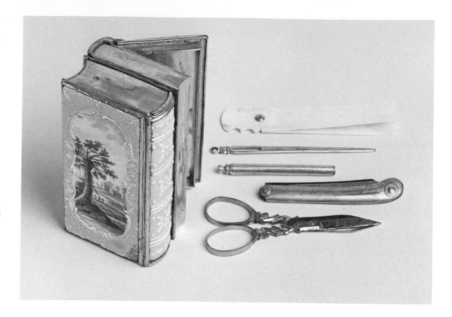

Right: An unusual *nécessaire* in the form of two books—one to be used as a box, the other fitted with ivory tablets, pencil, penknife, scissors and a bodkin. In the centre of each cover is a painted, pastoral scene, reserved within a pink background, with raised white rococo scrolled panels and enrichments on each spine. Probably made in Bilston around 1770. Height 8.2 cm (3¼ ins) (Wolverhampton Museum)

good Frederick the Great enamel snuff-box for £6 and later found another for £2.16s.

In a shop in Genoa she saw: 'two pretty specimens of Battersea enamel, one a green étui, the other a snuff box. They are upwards of £3.3s apiece. Too dear'.[3] Today, if in good condition, these two would probably be worth in excess of £500.

Following the death in 1884 of Charles Schreiber, Lady Charlotte devoted her days to cataloguing her vast collections. Her collecting years were over and in memory of her husband, she bequeathed over 1800 items of porcelain, pottery, glass and enamels to the South Kensington Museum; to the British Museum she gave her fans and playing cards. She died at the age of 83 in 1895.

Another fine and famous collection of English enamels was amassed with great expertise by the Hon. Mrs Nellie Ionides. Following her death in 1963, the collection was dispersed by bequests and by sales at auction. Although a group of important specimens was given to the Victoria and Albert Museum, this was a sad end to an incomparable collection but nevertheless it enriched a market which was by then depleted of these much-sought-after objects. Other fine collections similarly dispersed were those of the late Gerald Mander, Lord Ilford and Sir William Mullens.

Exceptional existing collections in England, amassed by connoisseurs now deceased, include those of Egan Mew (which now forms part of the superb, historically comprehensive, collection at Wolverhampton); the Raby Collection at the

Manchester Art Gallery, and the magnificent enamels collected by Queen Mary.

On a more modest scale, it is still possible to collect eighteenth-century and early nineteenth-century English enamels, but at a price. Small Bilston patch-boxes, which cost approximately £5 each in 1950 are, in 1978, worth upwards of £75. At auction, Battersea wine labels fetch around £400–£600 each. These prices reflect the tremendous upsurge that has taken place in the collecting of enamels.

Primarily, enamels are a good investment in times of inflation. Sotheby's have expressed the opinion that this is one of the few areas of antiques which is still undervalued in view of the scarcity which exists. Another possible reason that they are in such great demand is that many people who previously were unaware of the existence of this élitist group of objects have become interested in them as a result of the world-wide success of contemporary Bilston enamels, since the revival of the craft in 1970. This revival has brought enamels to the attention of untold numbers of new collectors and has activated in many a desire to acquire examples of the craft made in England two centuries ago.

In starting a collection it would be wise to bear in mind that eighteenth- and early nineteenth-century English enamels do not consist only of boxes. Indeed a great number and variety of interesting articles were made at the time and the items listed below may serve as a guide. Although many of them are very rare, it would be possible for the persevering collector, with the aim of forming a specialized collection, to choose from at least half this list. Having made the decision whether to seek one type of object or several, there are then endless refinements of subject, style, technique and period.

Below: Two embossed scent bottles in the Schreiber Collection which demonstrate how Chelsea toys were copied in enamel in the eighteenth century. The upper one is an original Chelsea porcelain scent bottle, modelled as a boy dressed as a gardener carrying a basket of fruit on his arm and another filled with flowers on his head. The lower enamel scent bottle is a copy made in South Staffordshire or in London. It has an inscription, *Pour les belles*, under the concave base. Height 9 cm (3½ ins) (Victoria & Albert Museum)

Articles to Collect

Badges	Crosses	Salt cellars
Beakers	Cutlery handles	Scent bottles
Bonbonnières	*Etuis*	Screwpegs
Bottle tickets	Games boxes	Sealing wax cases
Bowls	Hot water urns	Sewing accessories
Buckles	Inkpots	Snuff-boxes
Buttons	Inkstands	Sugar canisters
Caddy spoons	Jugs	Tea caddies
Candlesticks	Medallions	Tobacco boxes
Caskets	Mustard pots	Toilet boxes
Cassolettes	*Nécessaires*	Toothpick cases
Châtelaines	Nutmeg graters	Trays
Cloak pins	Patch-boxes	Vases
Cloakpegs	Perfume burners	Vinaigrettes
Coasters	Plaques	Watches and keys
Corkscrews	Powder bowls	Wax-jack holders
Counters	Quill pen stands	Wine funnels

Notes

Introduction
1 Rackham, B. Catalogue of the Schreiber Collection, Victoria & Albert Museum, London 1924, vol III; *Enamels and Glass* p. 5

History and Techniques of Enamelling
1 Snowman, A. K. *The Art of Carl Fabergé*, Faber & Faber, London, 3rd edition 1964, p. 53
2 Chambers, E. *Cyclopaedia*, 3rd edition, 1741, quoted by Eric Benton, English Ceramic Circle Transactions 8, 1972, pt 2, p. 149, note 3
3 Nightingale, J. E. *Contributions towards the History of Early English Porcelain from Contemporary Sources*, Salisbury 1881, p. IXV quoted by Charleston, R. J. E.C.C. Trans., vol 6, pt 2, 1966, p. 71
4 Watney, Bernard *Antiques International*, Spring Books, London, 1966, p. 287
5 Watney, Bernard E.C.C. Trans., vol 6, pt 2, 1966, p. 89
6 Hughes, T. & B. *English Painted Enamels*, Country Life, 1951, p. 36
7 *ibid*
8 Watney, Bernard E.C.C. Trans., vol 6, pt 2, 1966, p. 60
9 Hughes, T. & B. *English Painted Enamels*, p. 124

Manufacturing Processes
1 Hughes, T. & B. *English Painted Enamels*, p. 146

York House, Battersea
1 Sedgwick, Romney (Ed) *The History of Parliament, House of Commons, 1715–1754*, vol 11, Members E–Y, p. 171, H.M.S.O., London, 1970
2 Westropp, M. S. D. Proceedings of the Royal Irish Academy, Vol XXXII, C. no. 1, 1913, p. 7, quoted by Bernard Rackham, English Porcelain Circle Transactions no. IV, 1932, p. 73
3 Watney, Bernard. E.C.C. Trans., vol. 6, pt 2, 1966, p. 62
4 Quoted by Hughes, T. & B. *English Painted Enamels*, p. 51
5 *ibid*
6 Cook, C. E.C.C. Trans., vol. 3, pts 4 & 5, 1955, p. 191
7 Rackham, B. Catalogue of the Schreiber Collection, Victoria & Albert Museum, London, 1924, vol. III, p. 4
8 *ibid*, p. 6
9 *ibid*, p. 4
10 Gardener, H. *Art through the Ages*, Harcourt, Brace, Jovanovich, 6th edition, New York, 1975, p. 655
11 Mew, E. *Battersea Enamels*, The Medici Society, London, 1926, p. 22
12 Toppin, A. J. E.C.C. Trans. no. 9, vol. 2, 1946, p. 173
13 Sedgwick, R. (Ed). *The History of Parliament, House of Commons, 1715–1754*

London
1 Benton, E. E.C.C. Trans., vol. 8, pt 2, 1972, p. 163
2 Toppin, A. J. E.P.C. Trans., no. IV, 1932, p. 67–8
3 Smith, J. T. *Nollekens and his Times*, 1920 edition, vol. 1, p. 54, quoted by Claude Blair, Wartski Catalogue, *A Thousand Years of Enamel*, Exhibition, 1971
4 Heal, Sir A. *The London Goldsmiths*, 1200–1800, David & Charles, Newton Abbot, Devon, 1935
5 Rackham, B. E.P.C. Trans., no. IV, 1932, p. 68
6 Smith, J. T. *Nollekens and his Times*, quoted by Benton, E. E.C.C. Trans., 8, pt 2, 1972, p. 159
7 Foster, J. J. *A Dictionary of Painters of Miniatures*, Phillip Allan & Company, London, 1926, p. 65
8 Nightingale, J. E. *Contributions towards the History of Early English Porcelain from Contemporary Sources*, Salisbury, 1881, p. IXV quoted by Charleston, R. J. E.C.C. Trans., vol. 6, pt 2, 1966, p. 71

Birmingham
1 Watney, Bernard. E.C.C. Trans., vol. 6, pt 2, 1966, p. 64–5
2 Lord Fitzmaurice, *Life of William, Earl of Shelburne, I*, London, 1912, p. 398 ff, quoted by Charleston, R. J., E.C.C. Trans., vol. 6, pt 2, 1966, p. 79
3 Hutton, W. *History of Birmingham*, Pearson & Rollason, Birmingham, 1781, quoted by Watney, Bernard, E.C.C. Trans., vol. 6, pt 2, 1966, p. 64–5
4 Connell, B. *Portrait of a Whig Peer: . . . the Second Viscount Palmerston 1739–1802*, London, 1957, p. 26, quoted by Charleston, R. J. E.C.C. Trans., vol. 6, pt 2, 1966, p. 71
5 Journal of the House of Commons, 1759, quoted by Hughes, T. & B. *English Painted Enamels*, p. 79
6 Dickinson, H. W. *Matthew Boulton*, Cambridge, 1937, p. 121, quoted by Bernard Watney, E.C.C. Trans., vol. 6, pt 2, 1966, p. 65
7 Watney, B. E.C.C. Trans., vol. 6, pt 2, 1966, p. 61
8 Benton, E. E.C.C. Trans., vol. 7, pt 3, 1970, p. 162
9 Charleston, R. J. E.C.C. Trans., vol. 6, pt 2, 1966, p. 70
10 Hughes, T. & B. *English Painted Enamels*, p. 79
11 Watney, B. E.C.C. Trans., vol. 6, pt 2, 1966, p. 67
12 *ibid*, p. 90–1
13 Goodison, N. *Ormolu, the work of Matthew Boulton*, Phaidon Press, London, 1974, p. vii
14 Charleston, R. J. E.C.C. Trans., vol. 6, pt 2, 1966, p. 114

South Staffordshire
1 Benton, E. E.C.C. Trans., vol. 7, pt 3, 1970, p. 181
2 Hughes, T. & B. *English Painted Enamels*, p. 104
3 Watney, B. E.C.C. Trans., vol. 6, pt 2, 1966, p. 82, note 2
4 Hughes, T. & B. *English Painted Enamels*, p. 104–5
5 Hackwood, F. W. *Wednesbury Workshops, or some account of the industries of a Black country town*, Horton Bros., Wednesbury, 1889, quoted by Hughes, T. & B. *English Painted Enamels*, p. 105

Liverpool
1 Mayer, J. *The Art of Pottery; with a History of its Progress in Liverpool*, 1873, p. 54–7
2 Gatty, C. T. *The Liverpool Potteries*, Liverpool, 1882, p. 10, quoted by Turner, W. *Transfer Printing*, Chapman & Hall, London, 1907, p. 36

3 Mayer, J. *The Art of Pottery*, a paper read at Liverpool Museum on 1 March 1971, p. 41

Continental Painted Enamels
1 Ricketts, H. *Objects of Vertu*, Barrie & Jenkins, London, 1971, p. 75
2 Courajod, L. *Livre-Journal de Lazare Duvaux*, 2 vols, Paris, 1839

Fakes, Forgeries and Replicas
1 du Boulay, A. *Collecting The Times* July, 1976
2 Kurtz, O. *Fakes*, Dover Publications Inc., New York, 1967, p. 253

Decline and Revival of a Craft
1 Le Corbeiller, C. *European and American Snuff Boxes*, Batsford, London, 1966, p. 17

Collecting
1 Herrmann, F. *The English as Collectors*, Chatto & Windus, London, published in 1972, p. 334–43
2 Taken from an extract from *Lady Charlotte Schreiber's Journals*, vol. 1, contained in *The English as Collectors*, by Frank Herrmann
3 *ibid*

Glossary

Anneal To soften metal by heating and gradual cooling.

Bat printing Transfer printing by means of a sheet of glue called a 'bat', instead of paper.

Bezel A metal frame by which a watch dial or glass, or the lid of a box, is retained into its setting.

Bianco-sopra-bianco Raised white detail on a white enamel background.

Bibelots Curios, trinkets.

Black printing See Bat printing.

Blank A piece of metal or an undecorated object, prepared or formed and ready for further processing.

Bombé Convex, bulging.

Bonbonnière A container for sweetmeats.

Caillouté bleu nouveau A pebble design on a royal blue background.

Carnet-de-bal An ornamental case containing leaves, often of ivory, on which ladies wrote the names of their dancing partners.

Chamfered The surface produced by bevelling off a square edge.

Chase A method of working a pattern on metal whereby particles are not removed as they would be in engraving.

Chinoiserie European style of decoration using Chinese motifs, particularly popular from the second half of the seventeenth century to the early nineteenth century.

Coffin A case placed inside a kiln in which articles are fired.

Contre-émail Enamel on the reverse side of a piece which counteracts the tension of expansion and contraction of the enamel on the face during firing.

Diaper A design which consists of lines crossing diamond-wise, with motifs between the spaces.

Die An engraved or sculptured stamp for impressing a design or form onto a softer material.

Embossed Moulded in relief.

Etui A decorative container fitted with small personal accessories.

Fire To bake in a kiln or a furnace.

Fire-lute Tenacious, fireproof clay, used to seal the aperture of a coffin before placing it inside a kiln.

Flux Colourless enamel, before oxides are added for colouring.

Frit Enamel in the raw chunk or ground state.

Glaze On enamel, a vitreous transparent coating.

Grisaille Decoration in tones of grey.

Groundcoat enamel Foundation or undercoat of an enamel article, applied prior to cover-coating and decorating.

Japanned Lacquered or varnished with a hard, usually black, glossy finish.

Kiln A muffled furnace used for firing objects.

Medallion An oval or circular panel or tablet.

Mill A machine or apparatus for grinding a solid substance to powder.

Muffle An enclosed compartment within a kiln or furnace to protect contents from direct heat during firing.

Nécessaire A container fitted with small, useful articles such as sewing or writing accessories.

Opalescent enamel Enamel exhibiting a milky iridescence or play of colour similar to an opal.

Opaque enamels Enamels which obscure the ground onto which they are applied.

Patch Artificial beauty spot.

Pinchbeck An alloy, closely resembling gold, composed of approximately five parts of copper with one of zinc, invented by Christopher Pinchbeck, an eighteenth-century watchmaker.

Repoussé Metal raised into ornamental relief by means of hammering from the reverse side.

Reticulated Marked or decorated to resemble a net.

Rose-engine turned Curvilinear, intricate patterns engraved on metal by means of a tool attached to a turning lathe.

Scène grivoise Pornographic illustration.

Semi-opaque A stage between opalescent and opaque enamel, neither iridescent nor dense.

Size A glutinous wash which, when applied to a surface, provides a suitable ground to receive the inked design from a transfer or other decoration.

Slurry An opaque liquid mixture of enamel powder with water, less than 5% clay and a minimal amount of a chemical to render the liquid viscid.

Spike oil A distillation made from *Lavandula spica* (Lavender) employed in enamel painting which enables the enamel to spread but which burns away when fired.

Spinning The shaping of sheet metal by pressure applied during rotation on a lathe.

Stamping Shaping sheet metal by means of dies subjected to mechanical pressure.

Translucent or transparent enamel Enamel through which the background colour can be seen.

Vermiculé A term used to describe a type of ornamental work on a metal background, composed of sinuous lines reminiscent of the tracks of worms.

Vignette A small picture not enclosed in a border, its edges shading away.

Bibliography

Books

Blakemore, K. *Snuff Boxes,* Frederick Muller, London 1976

Cook, C. *The Life and Work of Robert Hancock,* Chapman & Hall, London 1948 and Supplement London 1955

le Corbeiller, C. *European and American Snuff Boxes,* Batsford, 1966

Cunynghame, H. H. *European Enamels,* Methuen, London, 1906

Goodison, N. *Ormolu: The Work of Matthew Boulton,* Phaidon, London, 1974

Hackenbrock, Y. *Chelsea and the other English Porcelain, Pottery and Enamels in the Collection of Irwin Untermeyer,* Thames & Hudson, London, 1957

Hughes, G. B. *English Snuff Boxes,* MacGibbon & Kee, London, 1971

Hughes, T. & B. *English Painted Enamels,* Country Life, 1951

Mayer, J. *The Art of Pottery: with a History of Its Progress in Liverpool,* 1873

Mew, E. *Battersea Enamels,* The Medici Society, London 1926

Moorhouse, J. *Collecting Oriental Antiques,* Hamlyn, Feltham, 1976

Ricketts, H. *Objects of Vertu,* Barrie & Jenkins, London 1971

Snowman, A. K. *The Art of Carl Fabergé,* Faber & Faber, London, 1964

Soame Jenyns, R. *Chinese Art, the Minor Arts,* Oldbourne Press, London, 1964

Turner, W. *Transfer Printing,* Chapman & Hall, London, 1907

Wilson, P. (Ed) *Antiques International,* Hamlyn, Feltham, 1973 (Watney, B. *English Enamels in the 18th Century,* p 287–96)

Catalogues

Catalogue to the Exhibition of English Painted Enamels at the Wolverhampton Art Gallery and Museum (written by Mary S. Morris) 1973

Catalogue to the Royal Leamington Spa Exhibition (written by Eric Benton) 1967

Catalogue to the Schreiber Collection, Victoria & Albert Museum, London, 1924; Enamels and Glass, vol III (written by Bernard Rackham)

Wartski Catalogue, A Thousand Years of Enamel Exhibition, London, 1971

Journals, Articles and Papers

Hayward, J. F. *Salomon Weininger, Master Faker,* The Connoisseur, London, November, 1974

Charleston, R. J., *Battersea, Bilston or Birmingham,* Victoria & Albert Museum Bulletin, vol III, no 1, Jan 1967

English Porcelain Circle Transactions:
Toppin, A. J. Notes on *Janssen and the Artists at the Battersea Factory,* no IV, 1932

English Ceramic Circle Transactions:
Benton, E. *John Brooks in Birmingham. The Bilston Enamellers,* vol 7, pt 3, 1970
Benton, E. *The London Enamellers,* vol 8, pt 2, 1972
Charleston, R. J. and Watney, B. *Petitions for Patents concerning Porcelain, Glass and Enamels with special reference to Birmingham,* vol 6, pt 2, 1966
Haggar, R. *Black-printing on Porcelain,* vol 10, pt 1, 1976

Acknowledgements

The author wishes to express her gratitude to Her Majesty the Queen and Her Majesty Queen Elizabeth, the Queen Mother for graciously allowing photographs of enamels from their collections to be included in this book. She is also indebted to the following who have generously given permission for their enamels to be illustrated in this book. Eric Benton, Lawrence Gould, M. Hakim, Bernard Watney, Michael Gillingham of John Sparks Ltd., Judith Moorhouse of Bluett and Sons Ltd., Kenneth Snowman of Wartski Ltd., Sotheby Parke Bernet & Co., the British Museum, the Merseyside Museum, the Victoria & Albert Museum, the Wolverhampton Museum and in the United States, Cartier, New York, the Horchow Collection, Dallas, Mr John C. Walsh and the Museum of the City of New York. For their invaluable assistance the author wishes to convey her appreciation and thanks to Mary Morris of Wolverhampton Museum, Julia Clarke of Sotheby Parke Bernet & Co., Jessica Jessel, Graham Thomas, Neal Hughes and his colleagues at Copper Enamels (Bilston) Ltd., and also to her associates at Halcyon Days.

The photographs in this book are by Prudence Cumings Associates except for the following; 8 (bottom) British Museum, John Freeman/Orbis Publishing; 15, 54 British Museum; 63 by gracious permission of H. M. the Queen. Copyright reserved; 6 Mansell Collection; 91 Merseyside Museum/Orbis Publishing; 121 Museum of the City of New York; 21, 87, 98 Sotheby Parke Bernet & Co.

The quotation on page 18 from *The Art of Carl Fabergé* by A. Kenneth Snowman is reproduced by kind permission of Faber & Faber Limited, London. We are also grateful to Faber & Faber Limited, London for permission to quote from Otto Kurz's book *Fakes* on page 104.

Index

London Printed, for Rob.t Sayer, Print & s